curriculum
connections

Civil War

Battles and Campaigns

BROWN
BEAR
BOOKS

Published by Brown Bear Books Ltd

4877 N. Circulo Bujia
Tucson
AZ 85718
USA

First Floor
9–17 St. Albans Place
London N1 0NX
UK

© 2011 Brown Bear Books Ltd

ISBN: 978-1-936333-43-1

Managing Editor: Tim Cooke
Designer: Joan Curtis
Picture Researcher: Sophie Mortimer
Art Director: Jeni Child
Editorial Director: Lindsey Lowe

Library of Congress Cataloging-in-Publication Data

Battles and campaigns / edited by Tim Cooke.
    p. cm. -- (Curriculum connections : Civil War)
Includes index.
 Summary: "In an alphabetical almanac format, describes the location, strategies, key players, and outcomes of many U.S. Civil War battles, campaigns, and plans"--Provided by publisher.
 ISBN 978-1-936333-43-1 (library binding)
1. United States--History--Civil War, 1861-1865--Campaigns--Juvenile literature. I. Cooke, Timothy, 1961- II. Title. III. Series.

 E470.B327 2012
 973.7'3--dc22

                    2011005392

Picture Credits

Cover Image
Robert Hunt Library

Library of Congress: 27, 30, 33, 45, 47, 54, 59, 68, 71, 76, 78, 93, 100; National Archives: 57; Robert Hunt Library: 12, 20.

Artwork © Brown Bear Books Ltd

Brown Bear Books Ltd has made every effort to trace copyright holders of the pictures used in this book. Anyone having claims to ownership not identified above is invited to contact Brown Bear Books Ltd.

Printed in the United States of America

Contents

Introduction

Civil War forms part of the Curriculum Connections series. Each of the six volumes of the set covers a particular aspect of the conflict: Home Front and the Economy; Behind the Fighting; Weapons, Tactics, and Strategy; Politics; Battles and Campaigns; and People.

About this set

Each volume in *Civil War* features illustrated chapters, providing in-depth information about each subject. The chapters are all listed in the contents pages of each book. Each volume can be studied to provide a comprehensive understanding of all aspects of the conflict. However, each chapter may also be studied independently.

Within each chapter there are two key aids to learning that are to be found in color sidebars located in the margins of each page:

Curriculum Context sidebars indicate to the reader that a subject has a particular relevance to certain key state and national history guidelines and curricula. They highlight essential information or suggest useful ways for students to consider a subject or to include it in their studies.

Glossary sidebars define key words within the text.

At the end of the book, a summary **Glossary** lists the key terms defined in the volume. There is also a list of further print and Web-based resources and a full volume index.

Fully captioned illustrations play an important role throughout the set, including photographs and explanatory maps.

About this book

Battles and Campaigns uses photographs and detailed battle maps to describe all of the most important military engagements of the war, from the First Battle of Bull Run (Manassas) in July 1861 to the surrender of the Confederate commander Robert E. Lee to his Union counterpart Ulysses S. Grant at Appomattox Court House on April 9, 1865.

While the South set out to invade the North, the North imposed a naval blockade on Southern ports and attempted an advance on the Southern capital, Richmond, by fighting along the Virginia Peninsula. In the early stages of the war, both sides suffered from poor leadership, in part due to the appointment of officers for their political loyalties rather than their military ability. As the conflict went on, so a generation of more able commanders emerged, including Lee and "Stonewall" Jackson in the South and Grant and William T. Sherman in the North.

The course of much of the fighting was dictated by the need to control vital railroad lines and rivers. The North realized that it could cut the Confederacy in two by capturing the Mississippi, Ohio, and Tennessee Rivers and rail junctions at Chattanooga. The Confederates meanwhile invaded the North on a number of occasions, but reached their "high-water mark" at Gettysburg in July 1863.

From then, the South was on the back foot. Lee fought a series of remarkable defensive battles while key Southern positions and cities were besieged. The fall of Atlanta and Sherman's "March to the Sea," in which Union troops devastated Southern territory, brought the Confederacy to its end—although, as this book reveals, some Southern commanders refused to lay down their arms for weeks after the surrender at Appomattox Court House.

Anaconda Plan

When war broke out on April 12, 1861, the Union had no overall strategy for defeating the Confederacy. The commander-in-chief of the U.S. Army, Winfield Scott, devised a plan that became known as the Anaconda Plan.

Scott outlined his strategy in a letter to Major General George B. McClellan on May 3, 1861. He did not propose an invasion of the South but a campaign to surround and isolate the Confederate states to deprive them of supplies and force a peace deal.

Naval blockade

Part of Scott's plan was already in action. On April 19 President Lincoln had ordered a naval blockade of the major Confederate ports. By the end of April the blockade was being established from Norfolk, Virginia, to Galveston, Texas. Scott proposed tightening the cordon to shut down the Confederacy's Atlantic trade.

Control of the Mississippi

Scott also proposed that the Union close off the western part of the Confederacy by gaining control of the Mississippi River. This would be achieved by capturing the forts in the Mississippi Delta, occupying New Orleans, and sending gunboats and an army of 60,000 men down the river from Illinois. Mastery of the river would cut off the Confederate states of Texas, Arkansas, and most of Louisiana from the rest of the South. It was a cautious, long-term strategy that relied for success on squeezing the South economically.

The thinking behind the plan

Scott decided on his plan for two reasons. He had a limited number of men: the army he commanded was tiny with only 16,000 professional soldiers, or "regulars." On April 15 Lincoln called on the Union states to recruit

Curriculum Context

The legality of Lincoln's decision to order a naval blockade without the initial approval of Congress was later challenged in the Supreme Court.

Curriculum Context

It might be useful to be able to describe the basic elements of the Union plan at the start of the war.

75,000 volunteer militia, but they were only to serve for three months. Scott doubted whether these "90-day men" could be relied on to fight a long campaign. The government promised an extra 25,000 regulars and 60,000 volunteers to enlist for three years, but that was not enough to defeat the Confederacy. The other reason for Scott's strategy was that he hoped to win the South back without destroying it. He understood the depth of hatred a civil war would create.

War fever

When the Northern press learned of Scott's idea, they ridiculed its caution, dubbing it "the Anaconda Plan" for a river snake that coils around its prey and squeezes it to death. The Anaconda Plan found little favor with Union politicians and army officers eager for a quick victory. Scott had foreseen this in his letter to McClellan: "The greatest obstacle in the way of this plan [is] the impatience of our patriotic and loyal Union friends. They will urge instant and vigorous action, regardless, I fear, of the consequences."

Scott was right. The North was gripped with war fever. In May the Confederacy had established its capital in Richmond, barely 100 miles (160 km) from Washington, and a Southern army was forming south of the Potomac at Manassas. The North was eager to strike at the Confederacy—"On to Richmond!" was the popular cry. By June 1861 the Anaconda Plan had been quietly dropped. In November Winfield Scott retired from the army and was replaced by his protégé McClellan.

Scott's plan to regain the Mississippi River was not rejected entirely. The campaign began in February 1862 with the first attack by generals John Pope and Ulysses S. Grant and the recapture of New Orleans in April 1862 by naval officer David G. Farragut. It proved a longer and bloodier business than Scott imagined, but played a vital part in the Union's final victory.

Enlist
To join the military services.

Curriculum Context

War fever in the Union came to an end after the shock of defeat in the First Battle of Bull Run (Manassas) in July 1861.

Antietam (Sharpsburg), Battle of

The Battle of Antietam, fought at Antietam Creek near Sharpsburg, Maryland, on September 17, 1862, was the climax to Confederate General Robert E. Lee's first invasion of the North. It was the bloodiest single day of the Civil War.

By the end of August 1862 the Army of Northern Virginia was positioned along the Potomac River and had defeated two separate Union armies. General Robert E. Lee wanted to keep the forward momentum of the army going and saw the chance to take the war into the Union states. He could not attack Washington, D.C., because its defenses were too strong, but he could invade neighboring Maryland. On September 4 the Army of Northern Virginia began crossing the Potomac at Leesburg.

Moving north into Maryland, Lee intended to cross South Mountain and advance on the towns of Boonsboro and Hagerstown. However, this would leave the Union garrison at Harpers Ferry in a dangerous position behind him. On September 9 Lee divided his army, sending over half of it, under his trusted General Stonewall Jackson, west to capture Harpers Ferry.

General George B. McClellan and the Army of the Potomac were by this time advancing north, and on September 13 a copy of Lee's orders fell into Union hands. McClellan now knew exactly where the Army of Northern Virginia was and how divided Lee's position was. On the 14th he attacked the Confederates at South Mountain. Lee realized that McClellan was advancing between the two halves of his army. On the 15th he ordered Jackson back from Harpers Ferry and pulled his own forces toward the Potomac. The Confederates would concentrate near Sharpsburg, between the Potomac and Antietam Creek.

Garrison
A unit of soldiers guarding a town or other stronghold.

South Mountain
The battle is described on page 89.

Lee's position on September 16 was not promising. He had only 18,000 men stretched along a 3-mile (5-km) long line on high ground above Sharpsburg, with his back to a bend of the Potomac River. The far left of the line lay along the Hagerstown Pike about 2 miles (3.2 km) north of the village of Sharpsburg at an area called the West, East, and North Woods. His far right lay barely a mile south of the village on the Harpers Ferry road. The center was split by the Boonsboro Pike. It was an exposed position, mostly running through cornfields and fruit orchards with little natural cover. Antietam Creek might have offered some defense, but it was crossed by three bridges and a number of fords. Lee's only line of retreat was over a single ford across the Potomac. Facing Lee was McClellan's army of more than 75,000 men advancing from the north and east.

Curriculum Context

It might be interesting to summarize the strengths and weaknesses of Lee's position.

Union attack

Fighting began at dusk on September 16 when Joseph Hooker's Union I Corps began attacking from the north down the Hagerstown Pike toward the North Woods. Stonewall Jackson and the first of his units had begun to arrive, and by nightfall the Confederates had repulsed Hooker's advance. The following morning at 6:00 A.M. McClellan began the battle in earnest with an artillery bombardment.

Hooker's corps attacked again. Ten brigades hit the Confederate left and pushed their line back to the West Woods. Jackson counterattacked at 7:00 A.M. and threw the Union forces back, but Hooker received reinforcements from Mansfield's XII Corps. The battle now centered on the struggle for the possession of the Dunker Church, which stood in the West Woods.

Brigade

A military unit consisting of between two and six regiments; the brigade was the most common tactical unit of the Civil War.

Three divisions of Sumner's II Corps came forward from the Union right to help Mansfield. Attacking into the West Woods, one of the divisions advanced straight into a line of Confederates and suffered more than

This map shows the respective Union and Confederate front lines early in the day at Sharpsburg and the line to which the Confederates fell back in the afternoon.

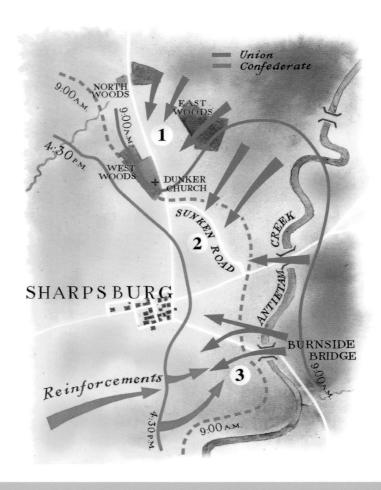

Battle Details

1. Union commander McClellan planned to attack both Confederate flanks at once. Union forces launched a dawn attack from the north on the Confederate left flank, and there was fierce fighting in the North, East, and West Woods and around the Dunker Church.

2. The battle shifted south to the center of the Confederate line. At the sunken road (later called Bloody Lane) Confederates held off repeated

Union attacks for nearly 4 hours. They were forced to retreat at about 1:00 P.M.

3. Ordered to attack the Confederate right flank at 8:00 A.M., Union commander Burnside crossed the creek and started his attack at 3:00 P.M., pushing the Confederates back toward Sharpsburg. The arrival of Confederate reinforcements forced the Union troops to retreat and ended the battle in a bloody draw.

2,500 men killed or wounded in 20 minutes, including General John Sedgwick, the division commander. Falling back nearly a mile, the Union troops took up defensive positions. The fighting for the West Woods was at a stalemate.

Bloody Lane

Meanwhile, another of Sumner's divisions lost its way and marched toward the Confederate center. At 9:30 A.M. it attacked brigades holding the sunken road that ran between the Boonsboro and Hagerstown Pikes, later called Bloody Lane. Fighting continued here for nearly four hours as first one Union division and then a second made repeated charges.

At about the same time on the right of the Union line IX Corps under Ambrose E. Burnside began attacking across the creek at the Rohrbach Bridge, later renamed Burnside Bridge. Burnside sent in brigade after brigade but was held off by a Confederate force of just 400 Georgians. They held the bridge until 1:00 P.M., when one of Burnside's division commanders had the good sense to use a nearby ford and flank the Confederate position.

By early afternoon the Confederate line was on the verge of collapse. Reinforcements had been arriving from Harpers Ferry all day. But Lee only had one division in reserve, and by noon he had committed most of that to help defend the sunken road. At 1:00 P.M. the sunken road fell to the Union, and the Confederates fell back toward Sharpsburg. By now most of Burnside's forces had crossed Antietam Creek. At 3:00 P.M. they started to advance.

McClellan hesitates

McClellan still had two army corps in reserve. If he had sent them forward, he would have won the battle—but instead he hesitated. His timidity cost the Union what

President Abraham Lincoln with General George B. McClellan (sixth from left) and other Union officers at Antietam.

Curriculum Context

Students assessing the most significant battles of the war should include Antietam (Sharpsburg) because it stopped the invasion of the North and allowed Lincoln to issue the Emancipation Proclamation.

would have been a great victory. As Burnside's men advanced, a sudden attack struck their left flank. Confederates who had marched from Harpers Ferry arrived at that moment to stop Burnside's attack and force it back toward the creek.

At nightfall the battle ended in a standoff among the dead and dying. Both armies had suffered terrible casualties. McClellan had lost 12,400 dead, wounded, or missing, while Lee had suffered more than 10,000 casualties. September 17, 1862, was the bloodiest day of the entire war. Although the battle was a draw in tactical terms, it was a strategic victory for the Union because the Confederate invasion of the North had been halted.

Lee considered counterattacking, but his officers argued against the idea. Both sides held their positions the next day. On the 19th Lee led his army back across the Potomac. President Lincoln interpreted the battle as a Union victory in order to issue his preliminary Emancipation Proclamation three days later.

Appomattox Campaign

The first days of April 1865 witnessed the last major campaign of the Civil War—and the final defeat of Robert E. Lee's Confederate Army of Northern Virginia. Lee surrendered his army to Union General Ulysses S. Grant on April 9.

By spring 1865 Union armies were in complete ascendancy in the eastern theater. In the Carolinas Union General William T. Sherman's March to the Sea had taken Charleston and the last Confederate port of Wilmington. His only opposition was the Army of Tennessee, under the command of Joseph E. Johnston. Johnston's force was a shadow of its former size, with just 15,000 foot soldiers plus a few thousand cavalry facing almost 90,000 in Sherman's army.

Meanwhile, in Virginia Union forces under Ulysses S. Grant had been besieging Petersburg since June 1864. Lee's Army of Northern Virginia was defeated by Grant outside Petersburg at Five Forks on April 1. Grant attacked the Petersburg defenses the following day. The Confederates began to retreat from Petersburg and their capital of Richmond on April 2 and 3. The Confederate situation was desperate.

Race to the west

Lee's weakened army raced west in an attempt to outpace the Union troops and meet with Johnston at Danville, planning to make a combined stand. Lee lost a day waiting for supplies for his hungry and tired men at Amelia Court House on the Richmond and Danville Railroad. The desperately needed supplies never arrived, and the soldiers searched in vain for food in the ravaged countryside nearby. On April 5 skirmishes broke out as Union cavalry and infantry harassed the Confederates in the area around Amelia Court House and Tabernacle Creek. Meanwhile, Union cavalry under

March to the Sea
You can read about Sherman's controversial campaign on pages 63–66.

Petersburg
The siege is described on page 75.

Curriculum Context

You might be asked to describe how shortages of supplies impacted the Confederate armies later in the war.

Sheridan had outpaced Lee and blocked his route south at Jetersville on the Richmond and Danville Railroad. Lee was forced to set out west for Farmville, ordering supplies to be sent from Lynchburg.

Flank

The exposed right or left hand wing of an army.

Union forces were closing in on the Confederate flank, and catching up to the army's rear. Lee led his men on a rapid night march west to Rice's Station on the Southside Railroad. Many sick and starving soldiers dropped out through sheer exhaustion.

After evacuating Petersburg and Richmond on April 2 and 3, Lee's exhausted Confederates struggled west, planning to meet with Johnston's army. Union forces overtook them, and Lee finally surrendered to Grant at Appomattox Court House on April 9.

Battle of Sayler's Creek

The straggling rear of the Confederate army was battered by a sustained assault from Union troops near Sayler's Creek on April 6. The fighting had a devastating effect. Between 7,000 and 8,000 of Lee's army—about one-third of those who had marched from Amelia Court House—were killed, wounded, or captured. Among those taken prisoner were six generals: Richard S. Ewell, George W.C. Lee, Joseph B. Kershaw, Montgomery Corse, Dudley M. duBose, and Eppa Hunton.

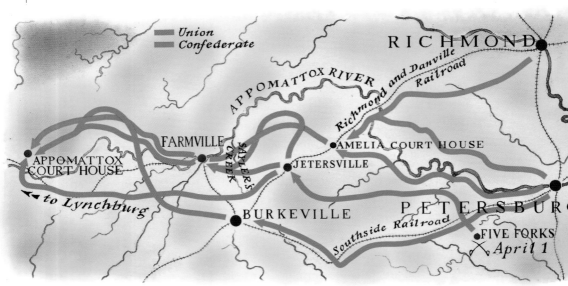

In one of the skirmishes that day a small Union force of about 600 infantry and cavalry was cut off at High Bridge, which took the Southside Railroad over the Appomattox River. They had hoped to destroy it and prevent Lee crossing, but failed. The officers leading the force, Theodore Read and Francis Washburn, decided that it was worth sacrificing the command in order to delay Lee's march. They repeatedly charged the advancing Confederate columns. Both the commanders and many of their men were killed in the courageous attempt.

Lee led his exhausted men over the Appomattox River on the 7th, now attempting to reach the town of Lynchburg. The Union troops gave chase. Confederate supplies had reached Appomattox Station, but Sheridan got there first and captured them. Lee found himself trapped between the Union forces of Sheridan, Humphreys, and Wright. He sent 1,600 infantry and 2,400 cavalry to try to fight a way through Sheridan's forces, but they had little success.

Lee surrenders

Some of Lee's junior officers now appealed to their commander to scatter his army. They believed that the South would be able to continue the fight using guerrilla warfare. Lee, however, realized that even if two-thirds of his 15,000 troops escaped—which was probably an over optimistic estimate—they would be an ineffective force scattered widely across the South. Lee saw that he had run out of military options and declared: "There is nothing left for me to do but to go and see General Grant, and I would rather die a thousand deaths."

At 1:00 P.M. on April 9—Palm Sunday—Lee rode to the small settlement of Appomattox Court House. There he surrendered the last great army of the Confederacy to Ulysses S. Grant.

Guerrilla warfare
Warfare that takes place through small-scale engagements, ambushes, and sabotage, rather than through set battles.

Curriculum Context
Students asked to describe the key moments of the conflict would usually include the Confederate surrender.

Atlanta, Fall of

The four-month struggle for Atlanta, Georgia, in 1864 was one of the war's most decisive campaigns. When it began in May, the Confederacy still had a chance to make good its independence. By the time it ended, that chance had gone.

Curriculum Context

You many be asked to understand the importance of Atlanta to the Southern economy, which had far fewer manufacturing centers than the North.

Nicknamed the Gateway City, Atlanta was a crucial Southern manufacturing and railroad center. Its factories produced a wide variety of military goods, including cannons, pistols, ammunition, uniforms, shoes, and naval armor plate. In symbolic importance to the Confederacy the city ranked second only to the capital of Richmond, Virginia.

The campaign for the city began on May 7, 1864, when three Union armies under William T. Sherman left Chattanooga, Tennessee, and Ringgold, Georgia. Sherman led 100,000 men. His opponent, Confederate General Joseph E. Johnston, had only about 60,000 men, but had the advantage of fighting on the defensive in mountainous country. Moreover, the farther Sherman advanced, the more difficulty he had in keeping his army supplied. Johnston hoped that by giving up ground he would gain time while he waited for an opportunity to counterattack. Sherman, for his part, hoped to sweep around the Confederate flank and trap Johnston in an isolated mountain valley.

Hood's campaign

Both commanders were frustrated. In the first two months Johnston had to abandon much more ground than he expected to yield, while Sherman could find no good opportunity to strike at Johnston's forces. The first major battle of the campaign took place on June 27, when Sherman hurled his army against an entrenched Confederate line on Kennesaw Mountain, about 20 miles (32 km) northwest of Atlanta. The Union

Kennesaw Mountain

Read details of the battle on page 62.

commander believed that Johnston's line was weak at that point. He was wrong and lost 3,000 troops in a series of doomed attacks. Confederate casualties numbered fewer than 1,000.

Sherman approaches Atlanta

After Kennesaw Mountain Sherman resumed his efforts to outflank Johnston's army. On July 8 he managed to cross the Chattahoochee River, the last natural barrier separating him from Atlanta. The city was now only 7 miles (11 km) away. Although Johnston remained unbeaten, Confederate President Jefferson Davis considered his defense too passive. On July 17 he replaced Johnston with John Bell Hood, a commander known for his fighting spirit and aggression.

Hood's campaign

Until Hood's appointment the campaign had been primarily one of maneuver; as soon as he took charge, it changed to one of headlong battle. Hood attacked part of Sherman's army at Peachtree Creek on July 20. He lost nearly 5,000 men compared with fewer than 2,000 Union casualties. Two days later he attacked

Outflank
To go around the side of an opposing force.

This photograph shows a railroad destroyed by Hood's Confederate troops during their retreat from Atlanta, in September 1864.

Curriculum Context

Siege warfare was a common tactic in the 19th century; officers still studied it at military academies.

Jonesboro

You can read about Jonesboro on page 61.

again in the Battle of Atlanta, losing 8,000 men. Battered by these defeats, Hood's army holed up in earthworks surrounding Atlanta.

Sherman did not try to storm the fortifications. Instead, he began a long-range bombardment of the city while he attempted to cut the Confederate supply lines south of the city with most of his army. August saw Sherman and Hood clash repeatedly with one another for control of the Macon and Western Railroad. Finally, on August 31 and September 1 the Confederates lost two critical engagements at Jonesboro, 15 miles (24 km) south of Atlanta. With these defeats went the Confederate grip on the railroad. Hood had no choice but to abandon Atlanta. Union forces occupied the city without a fight on September 3.

Possession of the Gateway City cost the Union 5,000 dead, 25,000 wounded, and 5,000 missing: a total of 35,000. Estimated Confederate losses were 3,200 killed, 19,000 wounded, and 13,000 missing; a total of 35,200.

Morale boost for the North

Morale in the North had been low after a summer of military setbacks and seemingly endless stalemate. In August 1864 President Abraham Lincoln believed he would lose his bid for reelection as president in November. News of Atlanta's capture electrified the Union. It was tangible proof that the Union was winning the war.

Politically, historians consider the fall of Atlanta to be the biggest single factor in ensuring that Lincoln won a second term as president. Economically, the Union victory deprived the Confederacy of a badly needed manufacturing and rail center. Strategically, it opened the Deep South to renewed Union offensives. Defeat at Atlanta was a blow from which the Confederacy never recovered.

Curriculum Context

Lincoln's opponent in the 1864 election was George B. McClellan, who was inclined to compromise with the South. What might have been the consequences if Lincoln had been defeated?

Brandy Station, Battle of

Brandy Station was the largest cavalry battle ever fought in North America. It took place in Virginia on June 9, 1863. Union cavalry acquitted themselves well against the forces of legendary Confederate commander J.E.B. "Jeb" Stuart.

In early June 1863 Confederate General Robert E. Lee was planning his second invasion of the North in less than a year. The Battle of Brandy Station interrupted his plans. Although it did not change the course of the invasion, it was significant in that it typified many of the changes that occurred in cavalry development during the war, particularly for the Union.

Curriculum Context

You could use Brandy Station as an example if you are asked to describe how warfare changed during the conflict.

Morning engagements

On the morning of June 9 two groups of Union cavalry under General Alfred Pleasanton crossed the Rappahannock River. They planned to rendezvous near Brandy Station and attack Confederates in the area. One group under John Buford surprised William Jones' Confederate cavalry in their camps near the river. The fighting grew intense as Jones and his men established a defensive position and held it until reinforcements arrived. Much of the fighting on this part of the battlefield took place dismounted, as Union and Confederate cavalrymen fought as infantry from behind stone walls.

Meanwhile, the other Union force of 5,000 men under David M. Gregg crossed the Rappahannock several miles south of Buford, split into two groups, and attacked toward Fleetwood Hill, site of the Confederate cavalry commander J.E.B. "Jeb" Stuart's headquarters. Gregg's attack forced Jones to fall back to Fleetwood Hill as well. In a smaller engagement 4 miles (6.5 km) south at Stevensburg, however, Union forces were unable to break through to assist Gregg's advance.

Curriculum Context

"Jeb" Stuart is a good example of a commander who shaped the course of the war: he became a hero in the South.

A Union army wagon park near Brandy Station, May 1863. Hundreds of wagons, carrying essential supplies, followed each army.

Fleetwood Hill became the scene of a remarkable battle, as thousands of cavalrymen participated in massed charges and countercharges, with neither side able to gain an immediate advantage. As the afternoon went on, however, the number of casualties grew, and the northernmost Union forces under Buford and Pleasanton began to withdraw across the Rappahannock, pushed on by a series of Confederate counterattacks. Union forces near Fleetwood Hill also began to withdraw, leaving Stuart's cavalrymen in possession of the field.

Jeb Stuart could legitimately claim victory in the Battle of Brandy Station. His troopers held their positions and inflicted almost twice as many casualties (866) as they suffered themselves (485). This was not the whole story, however. Stuart had carried out a grand review of his cavalry on the day before the raid and was taken by surprise by the bold Union attack. In spite of their final retreat, Pleasanton's Union cavalrymen had fought well. This battle, and a skirmish at Kelly's Ford along the

Review

A formal military ceremony in which forces are reviewed by an important person.

Rappahannock the previous March, signaled the great improvement of the fighting spirit and skill of the Union cavalry. It may also have led Jeb Stuart to undertake extra risks during the subsequent Gettysburg campaign to redeem his reputation.

Union cavalry

For the first two years of the conflict Union cavalry units had suffered from poor leadership and training and were completely outclassed by the Confederate cavalry. Many Union cavalrymen, born and raised in towns and cities, knew little about horses. Indeed, many had to learn to ride once they enlisted. In contrast, cavalrymen from the more rural South had more experience with caring for and riding horses. Also, many Confederate cavalrymen fought in their own localities, giving them a great advantage in an age when few detailed maps of the United States existed.

Improved skill

Over time the gap in quality between Union and Confederate cavalry units narrowed. By the time of the Battle of Brandy Station, Northern superiority in resources and manufactured goods allowed Union cavalry to be better armed and better supplied with mounts. The fighting spirit of the individual Union cavalryman was never in doubt either, and leaders such as Buford turned their units into successful combat forces. After June 1863 the cavalry played an increasingly effective role in the Union war effort.

Maps

Drawing maps of possible sites of conflict was the task of the topographical engineers.

Curriculum Context

Students might be asked to give examples of how the North's economic superiority impacted the war on the battlefield.

Bull Run (Manassas), First Battle of

The First Battle of Bull Run, also called the First Battle of Manassas, was fought on July 21, 1861, near Manassas Junction in northern Virginia. The battle was the first large-scale contact between the Union and Confederate armies.

Curriculum Context

Any list of significant turning points in the war should include the impact of the First Battle of Bull Run on how both sides saw the conflict.

In July 1861, with the Civil War only a few months old, both sides were convinced that the war would be short and relatively bloodless. The Union and Confederacy alike believed that their armies were superior in every way to their opponents', and that one grand campaign would decide the war in their favor. Prior to July 1861 the two adversaries had only fought a few small engagements. The First Battle of Bull Run showed both sides that the war would be long and bloody.

President Abraham Lincoln had raised a large army of volunteers after the Confederate bombardment of Fort Sumter, South Carolina, in April. By early summer he faced enormous popular pressure to send his armies to march on the new Confederate capital at Richmond, Virginia. The newspapers were full of the cry "Forward to Richmond!" Many volunteers had enlisted for only a year or less, increasing the pressure to secure a quick result. General Irvin McDowell, commander of the main Union force of 35,000 outside of Washington, protested that his army of citizen-soldiers was not trained or prepared for a campaign, but public demand was irresistible, and he was ordered to set out toward Richmond in early July.

Curriculum Context

Do you think that many Americans were unrealistic in how they saw the coming war?

McDowell's target was the equally inexperienced main Confederate army of 20,000, commanded by Pierre G.T. Beauregard, who had been McDowell's classmate at the military academy at West Point. Beauregard's army occupied a position just north of Manassas Junction only 30 miles (48 km) from Washington, along a small stream called Bull Run Creek. Manassas was a key Confederate supply depot and a stop on the railroad linking northern Virginia with the Shenandoah Valley to the west. In the Shenandoah Valley, meanwhile, Union General Robert Patterson, a veteran of the War of 1812 with 18,000 troops, had orders to prevent Confederate General Joseph E. Johnston moving his 12,000 men to support Beauregard.

McDowell began his grand movement on July 16. He aimed to capture a Confederate detachment at Fairfax Court House, northeast of Manassas. However, just as he had feared, his raw troops had trouble with even the simplest maneuvers. The Confederates at Fairfax escaped to the main lines at Bull Run as the Union forces approached.

Maneuvers
Infantry in the Civil War learned how to maneuver on the battlefield by constant repetition of drill to practice coordinated movements.

In response to McDowell's movement Beauregard requested that Johnston's army come to his aid. On July 18 Johnston's Confederates managed to give Patterson the slip and began using the Manassas Gap Railroad to reinforce Beauregard. By July 21 the two Confederate armies were united. The movement marked the first use of railroads for the purpose of battlefield maneuver in the history of warfare.

Curriculum Context

The use of the railroad was an important development for the future of warfare.

Preliminary skirmish

On July 18 elements of McDowell's and Beauregard's armies finally made contact at Blackburn's Ford, one of six crossing points of Bull Run. It was defended by troops led by James Longstreet, who later gained fame as one of Robert E. Lee's principal subordinates. In a skirmish that lasted most of the afternoon, Longstreet's troops repelled Union forces led by Daniel Tyler and kept their positions on the south side of Bull Run.

The armies spent the next two days organizing their troops and doing reconnaissance. Both McDowell and Beauregard determined on the same battle plan for

Battle Details

1. On July 18 a Union detachment probed the fords across Bull Run. It was repulsed in a sharp skirmish that lasted all afternoon.

2. On July 21 the main Union force made a flanking movement, crossing Bull Run at Sudley Ford at 9:30 A.M. Fighting in the morning centered on Matthew's Hill. The Confederates were pushed back to Henry Hill by late morning.

3. In the afternoon fighting continued on Henry Hill. The Confederates were reinforced, and Jackson counterattacked. By late afternoon the Union troops were in full retreat.

This map shows the key actions in the First Battle of Bull Run (Manassas).

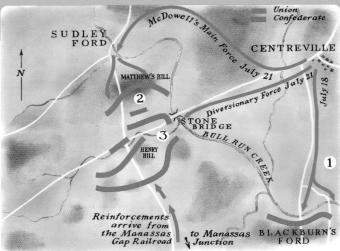

July 21—a turning of the enemy's left flank. McDowell planned to cross Bull Run via the Sudley Ford and position his army between those of Beauregard and Johnston, forcing both the Confederate forces to retreat. Beauregard also planned to attack his opponent's left flank. His network of spies in Washington had provided him with accurate information on the strength of the Union army.

Main battle

On the 21st McDowell was first to attack. As Tyler's men made a diversion in the center of the Confederate line, 13,000 men under David Hunter and Samuel Heintzelman made their way around the Confederate left flank and crossed Bull Run at Sudley Ford. A Confederate signal officer spotted the movement. In the war's first use of signal flags he alerted a force in time to send it to oppose the flanking movement. On Matthew's Hill Confederates from Georgia, South Carolina, Alabama, and Louisiana battled Union troops from Rhode Island, New Hampshire, and New York in a vicious struggle that marked the first experience of combat for many of the participants.

McDowell's army had the advantage of numbers and by late morning had pushed the Confederates back to a defensive position on Henry Hill. By the afternoon the Confederates were on the verge of defeat. The arrival of reinforcements, many from Johnston's Shenandoah Valley force, turned the tide. The Confederates were rallied by Thomas J. Jackson's Virginia brigade. It made a counterattack on the slopes of Henry Hill that earned Jackson his famous nickname of "Stonewall."

Other Confederate brigades attacked and pushed back McDowell's forces, who were exhausted by marching and fighting on a brutally hot day. By evening Union troops were in full retreat toward Washington. The retreat, initially reasonably orderly, descended into confusion as troops became entangled with the wagons of the many civilian spectators who had traveled from Washington, expecting to watch an easy Union victory. When the Confederates began to shell the road, the confusion developed into panic, and the disorderly retreat became a rout.

First Bull Run was small compared to later battles (1,900 Confederate and 2,800 Union casualties), but it was the first exposure to combat for many of the war's commanders. It proved the importance of railroads in troop movements and dispelled all illusions of a quick fight. The defeat was humiliating for the North who henceforth gave the war effort greater support.

> **Curriculum Context**
>
> The use of signal flags is another example of innovation in the Civil War.

> **Curriculum Context**
>
> Jackson's nickname came when other Confederates, trying to rally their men, shouted that Jackson's unit was standing "like a stone wall."

Bull Run (Manassas), Second Battle of

The Second Battle of Bull Run took place just over a year after the First Battle of Bull Run on the same battlefield. On August 29–30, 1862, John Pope's Union Army of Virginia fought Robert E. Lee's Confederate Army of Northern Virginia.

The Union commander, John Pope, planned to use his new Army of Virginia, combined with reinforcements from the Army of the Potomac, to attack the Confederate capital, Richmond, from the north. Pope, a brash general from the western theater, promised his troops that they would soon see the backs of their retreating enemies. Confederate General Robert E. Lee had recently completed his defeat of the Army of the Potomac in the Seven Days' Campaign of June 1862. However, Lee found himself in a strategically dangerous position. His army was positioned between the two much larger forces of McClellan and Pope. McClellan's forces were not yet ready to advance, however. Lee used the chance to confront Pope.

Lee's strategy

Lee devised a risky plan to deal with Pope, whom he personally disliked. In direct contradiction to accepted military strategy, he divided his forces, leaving a small detachment of his army outside Richmond to contain the Army of the Potomac. He sent "Stonewall" Jackson with 24,000 men to advance into central Virginia to confront Pope. Jackson defeated part of Pope's army at Cedar Mountain on August 9. Lee then rejoined Jackson with the rest of the army along the Rappahannock River.

Facing Pope across the river, Lee divided his army yet again, this time with the objective of defeating Pope's army before it could be reinforced by McClellan. Beginning on August 25, Jackson led 24,000 men

Seven Days' Campaign

This campaign is described on page 81.

Cedar Mountain

Read about the battle on page 29.

around Pope's right flank. Confederate General James Longstreet followed the next day. By nightfall on the 26th, after a 60-mile (96-km) march, Jackson had cut the Orange and Alexandria Railroad, Pope's supply line from Washington, and had seized and destroyed the Union supply depot at Manassas Junction.

Jackson then moved his force onto the site of the First Battle of Bull Run and waited for Longstreet. Pope moved to counter Jackson's flanking march, and the two forces clashed near Groveton, a few miles from Manassas, on July 28. The next day Longstreet arrived, and Lee's army was reunited.

The battle begins

The Second Battle of Bull Run began on August 29, on much of the same ground as the first battle in July 1861. Jackson entrenched his Confederates in the shelter of an unfinished railroad bed. They fought a desperate battle against attacking Union forces under Franz Sigel, Jesse L. Reno, and Samuel P. Heintzelman.

Confederate troops at Manassas Junction, having captured the Union supply depot on August 26, 1862. They feasted on the stores, then destroyed anything they could not take with them.

Entrench
To dig in to defensive positions.

At one point Confederate soldiers who had run out of ammunition resorted to throwing rocks at their adversaries. Their line held, however, because the Union attacks were poorly coordinated.

The second day's fighting opened with more Union attacks on Jackson's position at the railroad, this time by Fitz-John Porter's corps, sent to reinforce Pope from the Army of the Potomac. Meanwhile, Longstreet was preparing for a counterattack against the Union left flank. He launched his massive attack at 4:00 P.M., and the result was decisive. The Union left flank, completely unattended by Pope throughout the battle, was quickly crushed. Pope's army began withdrawing from the field. As night fell, a final Union position held firm on Henry Hill, site of the final Confederate defense a year earlier. This defense by part of Pope's force allowed the bulk of the army to escape. The next day Jackson attempted once again to encircle and cut off the Union army at Chantilly, but failed in a driving thunderstorm. Pope and his defeated army retreated to the fortifications around Washington.

Second Bull Run was the most complete of Lee's victories. At the cost of 9,500 casualties he inflicted 14,500 casualties on Pope's army and ended another Union attempt to capture Richmond. It was the high point of a summer that had seen Lee take command of the Army of Northern Virginia and defeat two Union armies. The initiative now in his hands, Lee decided to invade the North in hopes of another decisive victory. In September he took his army across the Potomac in a campaign that led to the Battle of Antietam.

Antietam

There is a description of the battle on pages 8–12.

Cedar Mountain, Battle of

A detachment of the Confederate Army of Northern Virginia under Thomas J. "Stonewall" Jackson clashed with part of John Pope's new Union Army of Virginia led by Nathaniel P. Banks on August 9, 1862, in Culpeper County, Virginia.

When Robert E. Lee contemplated his course of action following the Seven Days' Campaign in June 1862, he looked to one of his chief subordinates, Thomas J. "Stonewall" Jackson, to help him solve a strategic problem. As Lee faced the Union Army of the Potomac near Richmond, another Union army was forming under John Pope near Washington, D.C. A unit of this new Army of Virginia was led by a political appointee, Nathaniel P. Banks.

In late July Pope sent Banks with 12,000 soldiers to threaten the Virginia Central Railroad, a vital Confederate supply line. Lee reacted by sending Jackson with three divisions, totaling 22,000 troops, to deal with Banks. Jackson and Banks were old rivals. A few months earlier the two generals had faced off in the Shenandoah Valley. Now Jackson relished the chance to strike at his Union enemies again. On August 9 he positioned his troops on the northwest of Cedar Mountain in anticipation of a battle.

The day of battle

Jackson had outmaneuvered and defeated Banks before, but this time the battle began differently. Jackson's secretiveness over his orders caused confusion, and the Confederate forces arrived on the battlefield in a piecemeal condition. Jackson himself added to the confusion by spending hours placing artillery pieces on the right side of his line. Charles S. Winder was left to deploy his division on the Confederate left flank in a stand of trees.

Political appointee
A military officer given his commission early in the war because of his social position or political loyalties rather than for his military skill.

Deploy
To arrange soldiers in formation ready for battle.

The artillery of both sides began the battle and carried out an inconclusive duel while the infantry forces deployed. Banks attacked the left of Jackson's infantry line as it was forming. Winder was killed almost immediately, and his troops crumbled in the face of an energetic Union attack from a unit only a fraction of their size. For a time the Confederate position was critical, as the advancing Union forces under Samuel J. Crawford threatened to separate Winder's and Jubal A. Early's divisions from that of Ambrose P. Hill, which was still arriving on the field. On the march to Cedar Mountain, Hill and Jackson had quarreled, but this disagreement was forgotten for the moment. The arrival of Hill's division turned the tide. His five brigades made it to the field and marched straight into battle.

The Confederates rally

In a stirring display of bravery Jackson rallied his retreating troops in person. At one point he tried to pull his sword from its scabbard, only to find that it had

Union General Samuel J. Crawford's brigade advances at the Battle of Cedar Mountain. Greatly outnumbered, the brigade's determined attack almost prevailed against the Confederate forces.

rusted in place. Removing his sword and its scabbard from his belt and brandishing it in the air, he then took a battle flag from a soldier and waved it, shouting, "Jackson is with you!" His example, combined with arriving reinforcements, changed temporary Union success into defeat. The attacking Union forces, tired and disorganized from marching and fighting on a hot day, gave way before the Confederate counterattack and left the field by nightfall. At a cost of 1,400 casualties Jackson's force had defeated Banks and his men, inflicting 2,500 Union casualties in the process.

Although Jackson later declared that Cedar Mountain was "the most successful of his engagements," it was actually Hill's counterattack that led to victory. Jackson's own faulty dispositions and failure to attend to his left flank had almost cost him defeat at the hands of an enemy whom he outnumbered by two to one.

Two days later Jackson fell back to his base at the railroad junction at Gordonsville, where he awaited the arrival of Lee and the rest of the Army of Northern Virginia. Lee, Jackson, and James Longstreet were reunited on August 15 and began planning a strike against the rest of Pope's Army of Virginia. This resulted in the campaign and battle of Second Bull Run at the end of August 1862.

Curriculum Context

Despite the errors he made at Cedar Mountain, Jackson's bravery made him a popular hero in the South; when he died after being accidentally shot by Confederates in May 1863, it was a huge blow to Confederate morale.

Bull Run

Read about the battle on pages 26–28.

Chancellorsville, Battle of

The Battle of Chancellorsville saw Robert E. Lee's Confederate Army of Northern Virginia fight the Union Army of the Potomac led by Joseph Hooker on May 1–4, 1863. The battle is often regarded as the best example of Lee's tactical brilliance.

Through the winter of 1862–1863 the Union Army of the Potomac and the Confederate Army of Northern Virginia faced one another across the Rappahannock River at Fredericksburg, Virginia. The Union army had failed to take the city in a disastrous battle in December 1862. Union morale improved with the appointment of a new commander, Joseph Hooker, in January 1863.

Hooker's plan

Hooker reorganized the army and came up with a new plan of campaign for the spring. Instead of attempting a frontal attack on the Confederate positions that overlooked Fredericksburg, Hooker divided his army and took half of it—three corps totaling 75,000 men— to cross the river at fords upstream and come around in a wide sweep to attack Lee's army from behind. John Sedgwick stayed at Fredericksburg with 40,000 men to hold the Confederates.

By April 30 the Union troops had crossed the river and were in a dense area of woodland called the Wilderness. The center of their position was a crossroads at Chancellorsville, Virginia. Hooker's plan had worked smoothly so far, but now things started to go wrong.

Lee realized that Hooker was trying a flanking march. On April 29 he sent two brigades toward Chancellorsville to discover the size of the threat. Once they confirmed the Union army was at Chancellorsville,

Fredericksburg

The story of the battle is told on pages 47–49.

Curriculum Context

As the war went on, commanders looked for new alternatives to frontal attacks.

he went on the attack. Like Hooker, Lee divided his forces, leaving 10,000 men under Jubal A. Early to hold Fredericksburg and marching his remaining 50,000 men west to meet Hooker.

Hooker was taken by surprise on May 1 when the Confederates started an attack on his lead divisions at noon. The Union commander began to lose his nerve. In midafternoon he halted the advance and ordered his forces back to Chancellorsville to take up defensive positions.

Jackson's flanking march

Lee now had the initiative. In one of the war's boldest tactical moves he divided his army once again early on May 2. He sent Thomas J. "Stonewall" Jackson and 28,000 men on a 12-mile (19-km) march to strike Hooker's right flank, while his remaining troops faced three Union corps.

The march took all day, but at 6:00 P.M. Jackson attacked the Union XI Corps, which broke and ran. Only nightfall saved Hooker's army. That evening Jackson was shot by his own men, who mistook his party for Union cavalry. J.E.B. Stuart temporarily took over Jackson's command and on May 3 reopened the attack

The shooting of Stonewall Jackson on May 2 during the Battle of Chancellorsville. He was accidentally shot by his own men as he returned to his lines in the evening. His arm was amputated, but he died a few days later.

while Lee struck from the south. The Union line was pushed back from Chancellorsville north toward the river. Hooker was stunned when a shell exploded near him, and he handed command to Darius Couch.

The Union troops were facing total defeat. However, at Fredericksburg on May 3 the remaining Union troops under Sedgwick had attacked and driven away Early's troops. Sedgwick now advanced west to come to Hooker's aid. With Hooker in retreat on May 4 Lee turned to attack Sedgwick. At Salem Church the Confederates halted the Union advance.

Hooker withdrew across the river on the night of May 5. His defeat by an army half his size cost more than 17,000 casualties. Lee's losses were 12,800, including the irreplaceable Jackson, who died a few days later.

Curriculum Context

Jackson's death was a huge blow to morale in the South. Robert E. Lee said of his death that "I have lost my right arm."

Battle Details

1. In a brilliant maneuver the Union army marched north from Fredericksburg, crossed the river, and took up positions around the Chancellorsville crossroads by April 30.

2. On May 2 Jackson surprised and routed the Union right flank.

3. On May 3 fighting took place at both Chancellorsville and Fredericksburg, where Union forces attacked and drove the Confederates away and advanced to Salem Church.

4. Lee turned his army around to stop this advance and defeated the Union troops. On May 5 and 6 Union forces retreated across the river.

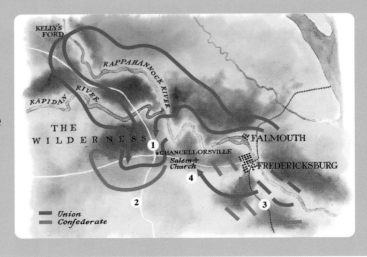

Chattanooga, Battle of

The city of Chattanooga, Tennessee, assumed great strategic importance for both sides during the Civil War. The fight to gain control of the city began in June 1863, culminating in the Battle of Chattanooga on November 23–25.

Chattanooga in southeastern Tennessee lay at the rail junction linking Virginia with Tennessee, Georgia, and points west. Without this vital rail terminus Confederate troops moving between different theaters of war would have to use a roundabout series of railroads in the Deep South. For the Union, on the other hand, Chattanooga was an objective because it could serve as a base for an attempt to capture Atlanta. As the war went on, it became clear that whoever controlled Chattanooga was in a position to control Tennessee, Georgia, and Alabama.

Union occupation

Between June and August 1863 Union General William S. Rosecrans and his Army of the Cumberland had opened up central and eastern Tennessee and driven Confederate General Braxton Bragg and his Army of Tennessee out of Chattanooga. The Confederates checked the Union advance at the Battle of Chickamauga (September 19–20), forcing the Army of the Cumberland back to Chattanooga. Bragg then laid siege to the city.

The outlook for the Union forces was grim, as their supplies quickly began to run out. The Confederates were unable to muster the strength to attack, however, and Lincoln reinforced the city with additional troops. In October Ulysses S. Grant arrived to resolve the situation. He reinvigorated his forces by restoring their supply lines and making efforts to dislodge the Confederates from the fortifications around the city.

Curriculum Context

Much of the strategy in the Civil War was dictated by the need to control railroads.

Curriculum Context

The Battle of Chickamauga is described on pages 38–39.

The "Battle above the Clouds"

On November 23 the Army of the Cumberland crossed the Tennessee River at several points in an attempt to break the Confederate siege. The offensive succeeded. Elements of Grant's army scaled Lookout Mountain despite the thick fog, forcing back Confederate forces

Battle Details

1. On October 26 Union forces established the "cracker" line to supply the Army of the Cumberland besieged in Chattanooga.

2. On November 23 Union troops dislodged the Confederates from their position on Orchard Knob, a foothill below Missionary Ridge.

3. Union troops then attacked Lookout Mountain in thick fog on November 24 and drove away Confederate forces.

4. Union forces converged on Missionary Ridge on November 25 and by 4:00 P.M. had routed Bragg's Confederates.

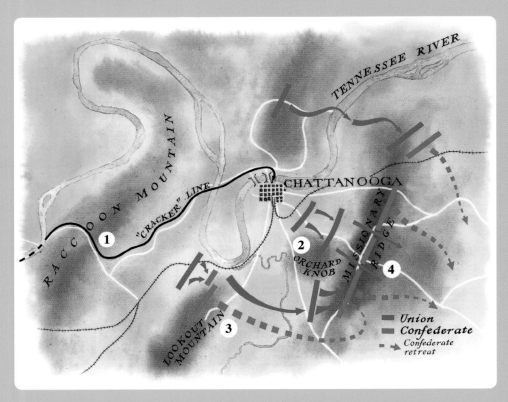

on November 24 in what became known as the "Battle above the Clouds". It succeeded in forcing Bragg out of a key position above Chattanooga.

Missionary Ridge

Following defeat at Lookout Mountain, Bragg entrenched on Missionary Ridge, a strong position stretching south from the Tennessee River. Bragg's generals placed their men in poor positions, however. In one of the war's most stunning victories, Union troops under George H. Thomas stormed Missionary Ridge on November 25 and defeated the Confederates. With no safe positions left, Bragg retreated south along the rail line to Atlanta in order to protect that key supply artery.

Union victory

The battles for Chattanooga were over. In six months Union armies had taken control of the "Gateway to the South" and changed the course of the war. Union forces under William T. Sherman now had the supply base and jumping-off point they needed to initiate a campaign against Atlanta.

For the Confederacy, meanwhile, the loss of Chattanooga completed their loss of the rail networks, food supplies, and manpower of central Tennessee.

Entrenched
Dug into defensive positions such as trenches and earthworks.

Curriculum Context
Sherman's subsequent assault on the South highlights how much of a turning point the Battle of Chattanooga was.

Chickamauga, Battle of

The Union Army of the Cumberland, commanded by William S. Rosecrans, fought Braxton Bragg's Confederate Army of Tennessee at Chickamauga on September 19–20, 1863. The battle was part of the campaign to gain control of Chattanooga.

Rosecrans's Union Army of the Cumberland forced Bragg's Confederates out of central Tennessee in the Tullahoma Campaign of June 1863. The Confederates fell back to Chattanooga, in southeastern Tennessee, a key rail junction. After Union victories at Gettysburg and Vicksburg the administration hoped the capture of Chattanooga would finish off the Confederacy. In an almost bloodless campaign Rosecrans's army managed to compel Bragg to evacuate the city on September 7. Bragg withdrew to northern Georgia, to Lafayette, and prepared to make a counterattack.

The armies maneuver

Rosecrans left a small force in Chattanooga and moved a 62,000-strong army southward into northern Georgia, believing Bragg was still in retreat. The three Union army corps became separated during the movement. Bragg saw his opportunity to strike at Rosecrans and moved west. Rosecrans, sensing danger, ordered his army to concentrate closer to Chattanooga. Meanwhile, Bragg was reinforced by two divisions under James Longstreet, bringing his total strength to 65,000.

As the Union army moved north on September 18, Rosecrans ordered George H. Thomas to position his corps north of Thomas L. Crittenden's corps to stop Bragg cutting off the Union army from Chattanooga. Not realizing that Thomas now formed the left flank of the Union army, Bragg's forces crossed over Chickamauga Creek and camped on the night of September 18.

The opposing battle lines were set, but due to the thickly wooded terrain along the creek, neither side was aware of the other. A single Union division initiated the battle the next morning. It advanced, believing that it had trapped a small Confederate force west of Chickamauga Creek. The fighting was confused and inconclusive, with both sides suffering heavy casualties.

Final day of battle

Bragg planned an attack to force the Union army south, away from Chattanooga and toward destruction. Initial Confederate attacks on the 20th began four hours late and made little headway against Thomas's defensive line on the Union left. At 11:00 A.M. Rosecrans made a critical mistake when he pulled Thomas Wood's division out of the right of his line to plug what he thought was a gap farther north. In fact, there was no gap until the moving of Wood's division created one. Fortunately for the Confederates, three of their divisions launched an attack into the gap at precisely the same time. Before Rosecrans could correct his mistake, the Union's defensive position was shattered. As Longstreet's men came close to cutting his line of communication with Chattanooga, Rosecrans ordered a retreat.

The "Rock of Chickamauga"

Troops under George H. Thomas made a stand on Snodgrass Hill, a ridge on the northern end of the Union line. In one of the war's most heroic defensive stands Thomas and his force held Bragg at bay as the bulk of the Union army withdrew into Chattanooga. For his efforts Thomas earned the Medal of Honor and was forever known as the "Rock of Chickamauga." Rosecrans was inconsolable as he was carried into Chattanooga by his army. Chickamauga was a hollow victory for the Confederates, however. At a cost of more than 18,000 casualties, Bragg had only pushed Rosecrans back to Chattanooga: he was unable to destroy him or force the surrender of his army by a siege.

Line of communication
The means by which commanders keep in touch with their armies, by telegraph or messengers.

Curriculum Context
If you are asked to highlight individual acts of bravery, Thomas' stand at Chickamauga could be included.

Cold Harbor, Battle of

Fought between June 1 and 3, 1864, in central Virginia, the Battle of Cold Harbor took place a month into the Union Army of the Potomac's campaign to attack the Confederate army while moving toward the Confederate capital, Richmond.

Curriculum Context

Although the South's defeat had become virtually inevitable, Lee cemented his reputation as the war's greatest commander with his attempts to defend Richmond.

The Army of the Potomac was commanded by George G. Meade, but the Union's general-in-chief, Ulysses S. Grant, planned and directed the campaign. In May 1864 Grant tried three times to crush Robert E. Lee's Army of Northern Virginia, at the Wilderness (May 5–6), Spotsylvania (May 10–12), and North Anna River (May 25–26). Each time Lee avoided defeat and withdrew to stand between Grant and Richmond. By May 29, however, the Army of the Potomac was just 11 miles (18 km) northeast of Richmond. Lee had Grant's line of march south covered, but to the east, on his far right flank, lay the Cold Harbor crossroads.

Strategic position

Named for an old tavern, Cold Harbor was only a few miles north of the Chickahominy River, the last natural obstacle between the Union troops and Richmond. If Grant gained control of the river, his route south was open once again. His far left flank was at Bethesda Church, several miles north of Cold Harbor. Both Grant and Lee saw that Cold Harbor was a strategically important position and began to concentrate their armies around it.

The Union gained the first success. On May 31 two cavalry divisions under Philip H. Sheridan advanced south from Bethesda Church and drove off Confederate cavalry holding the Cold Harbor crossroads. They were then counterattacked by two divisions of infantry ordered up by Lee. Meade told Sheridan to hold the crossroads "at all hazards" and ordered the Union VI

At all hazards

At any cost.

Corps to Cold Harbor to support Sheridan. After an overnight march of nine hours, VI Corps relieved the cavalrymen and secured the crossroads by 9:00 A.M on June 1.

Throughout the next two days both armies adjusted their battle lines. By June 2 a 7-mile (11-km) front had formed, extending from Bethesda Church to the Chickahominy River, with Cold Harbor in the center. Lee's 58,000-strong army was in position first. Late on

Battle Details

On May 31 Union cavalry captured the Old Cold Harbor crossroads from Confederate cavalry. Two divisions of Confederate infantry counterattacked, but Union reinforcements secured the crossroads by the morning of June 1.

There was some fighting on the next two days, but both armies spent much of their time adjusting their battle lines.

Early on June 3 Union troops launched their major attack. They suffered losses of about 7,000 troops in just 20 minutes. Stunned, they were unable to continue

their assault. Grant arrived on the battlefield at midday and called off the attack. The two sides dug in, and both stayed in position until June 12, when Grant began to withdraw his troops.

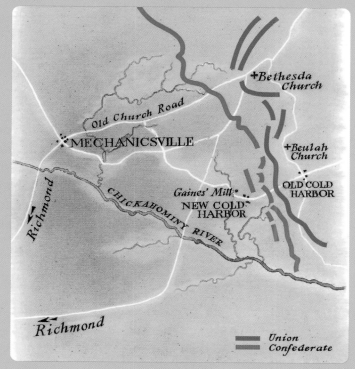

This map shows the two front lines at the start of the fighting on June 3.

June 1 two Union corps launched a fierce attack but were repulsed. Grant's army of five corps—more than 112,000 men—took longer to maneuver into position, marching on unfamiliar roads in the heat and dust.

Major attack

The major Union attack began at 4:30 A.M. on June 3. It was a disaster from the start. Only three corps at the southern end of the Union line pressed forward. They were met by a devastating crossfire from entrenched Confederate infantry and artillery. One division alone lost more than 1,000 men. A Union captain remembered that "the dreadful storm of lead and iron seemed more like a volcanic blast than a battle." One Confederate general just called it murder.

Within half an hour the assault stopped under the sheer weight of fire, but Grant did not call off the attack until midday, ordering his men to dig in where they could. The two armies confronted each other along these battle lines until June 12. Grant later wrote that he regretted that the last attack at Cold Harbor was ever made.

Cold Harbor cost the Union army 7,000 casualties for no gain at all. The Confederates only suffered about 1,500 casualties. Lee had held Grant once again, but despite the slaughter could not stop the Union advance. On June 12 Grant began to withdraw his troops and advance once again toward the south, crossing the James River to threaten Petersburg.

Crossfire

Enemy fire coming from both sides at the same time.

Curriculum Context

The combination of high casualties and little gain at Cold Harbor was a foretaste of the trench warfare of World War I (1914–1918).

Fair Oaks (Seven Pines), Battle of

The Battle of Fair Oaks, also called Seven Pines, took place outside Richmond, Virginia, on May 31 and June 1, 1862. It was the first major battle between the Confederate Army of Northern Virginia and the Union Army of the Potomac.

By May 1862 George B. McClellan's Union Army of the Potomac had reached the outskirts of Richmond, the Confederate capital. McClellan split his army, with two corps south of the Chickahominy River and three corps to the north, where they could join Union forces from Fredericksburg. Confederate commander Joseph E. Johnston would strike while the Union army was split. He had 75,000 troops available, while the two Union corps had only 31,500 troops under generals Erasmus D. Keyes and Samuel P. Heintzelman south of the river.

Confederate attack

Johnston's plan to advance in four columns along three roads that met at Keyes' isolated position at Seven Pines was sound, but he gave his orders orally, leading to confusion and delay. In addition, heavy rain turned the area into a bog. On May 31 Confederate General James Longstreet took his troops along a road assigned to other divisions, creating more chaos and weakening the assault. After a six-hour delay, only six of the 13 Confederate brigades were in position when the battle began. A Confederate assault pushed back Union troops to a third defensive line by evening. At around 7:00 P.M. Johnston was wounded, and General Gustavus W. Smith took charge. He renewed the Confederate attack the next day with poorly organized assaults, which were repulsed. President Davis replaced Smith as commander with Robert E. Lee, who immediately ordered a general withdrawal. The outcome of the battle was inconclusive. The Confederacy suffered about 6,150 casualties to the Union's 5,050 casualties.

> **Curriculum Context**
>
> You could use Seven Pines as an example to illustrate how battles could easily become confused.

Five Forks, Battle of

The Battle of Five Forks took place on April 1, 1865, at a crossroads near Petersburg, Virginia. It brought about the end of the Siege of Petersburg and marked the beginning of the end for Robert E. Lee's Army of Northern Virginia.

Curriculum Context

The defeat of Lee's Army of Northern Virginia would effectively mark the defeat of the South.

As the Virginia weather began to improve in late March 1865, and muddy roads began to dry out and harden, Union General Ulysses S. Grant, who was besieging the Confederate-held city of Petersburg, feared that his adversary, Confederate General Robert E. Lee, would attempt to evacuate the city's defenses and escape westward in order to join a Confederate army in North Carolina. To prevent Lee's escape, Grant planned an offensive that would cut off Lee's remaining escape routes to the west.

Key location
On March 31 elements of the Union Army of the Potomac under Philip H. Sheridan fought a sharp engagement with George Pickett's Confederates at Dinwiddie, west of Petersburg.

After the fighting Pickett withdrew to a hamlet known as Five Forks, from which five different roads radiated like spokes on a wheel. One road led directly north to Lee's last remaining supply line, the Southside Railroad. Lee ordered Pickett to hold Five Forks "at all hazards," and Pickett set about building fortifications to shelter his small force of infantry and cavalry.

At all hazards

At any cost.

Sheridan attacks
Union forces renewed the assault the next day, April 1. After moving stealthily into position, at 4:00 P.M. Sheridan's forces crashed out of the pine thickets and broke through the undermanned Confederate line in several places, killing and capturing thousands of

enemy troops. During the battle Pickett was absent attending a picnic with some of his fellow generals, so he did not know anything about the defeat until the survivors began streaming past him. By then it was too late for him to restore the situation, and he joined in the retreat.

On receiving word of the conclusive defeat at Five Forks, Lee was forced to make preparations to evacuate Petersburg. Grant, on the other hand, planned a climactic assault. On April 2 the Union assault caved in the Petersburg defenses.

At Five Forks the Confederates were routed by Union troops led by General Philip H. Sheridan.

While the Battle of Five Forks alone did not end the Petersburg campaign, the disastrous defeat helped seal the fate of Lee's Army of Northern Virginia.

Franklin, Battle of

The battle fought near Franklin, Tennessee, on November 30, 1864, was one of the most hotly contested engagements of the war. John Bell Hood's Confederate Army of Tennessee fought Union troops led by John M. Schofield.

The battle was part of the Nashville Campaign, the Confederate army's desperate attempt to retake Tennessee and force Union troops to withdraw from the Deep South. On November 29, 1864, John Bell Hood's 38,000-strong Confederate Army of Tennessee had narrowly missed trapping the smaller 27,900 Union force of John M. Schofield at Spring Hill. Furious that Schofield's retreating army had eluded him, Hood ordered his men to make a frontal assault on the Union troops entrenched outside the town of Franklin, Tennessee, the following day, November 30.

Confederate attack

As the sun set, with battle flags flying and bands playing "Dixie," Hood's soldiers made their charge. Well-directed Union rifle and artillery fire broke up the Confederate attacks on the right and left flanks. In the center the Confederates came very close to breaking the Union ranks. Bloody hand-to-hand fighting ensued in the trenches. At one point the Confederates charged through the trenches of an inexperienced Union regiment, sending them into flight. Only a well-timed counterattack saved the Union line. The fighting continued until about 9:00 P.M., when Hood ordered his men to withdraw. The attack cost his army dearly. More than 6,200 Confederates were killed, wounded, or captured. Among the dead were six generals, including Patrick Cleburne, the "Stonewall of the West." At night Schofield abandoned the field and continued his retreat to Nashville. The Union troops were followed by Hood's much weakened and dispirited Confederates.

Dixie

An unofficial anthem of the Confederacy, "Dixie" was an 1850s' popular song in which a freed slave looks back to the idealized plantation days of his childhood.

Nashville

Read about the end of the Nashville campaign on pages 70-71.

Fredericksburg, Battle of

In the depths of winter, on December 13, 1862, the Union Army of the Potomac under its new commander, Ambrose E. Burnside, attacked Robert E. Lee's Confederate Army of Northern Virginia at Fredericksburg, Virginia.

On November 7, 1862, President Abraham Lincoln appointed Ambrose E. Burnside commander of the Union Army of the Potomac in place of George B. McClellan, who he felt was not aggressive enough. Eager to prove his aggression, Burnside planned a winter offensive toward Richmond, Virginia, aiming to cross the Rappahannock River at Fredericksburg.

Burnside's movements

Burnside had a huge army of some 120,000 men. He reorganized it into three Grand Divisions—Right, Center, and Left—each of two army corps plus attached cavalry. By November 19 the Union army was occupying Falmouth to the north of Fredericksburg

A lithograph of the Union Army of the Potomac crossing the Rappahannock River to Fredericksburg under fire from Confederate snipers in December 1862.

Pontoon bridges

Temporary bridges, which often float on moored boats, or pontoons.

Curriculum Context

The delay in building bridges at Fredericksburg is an illustration of how a technological failure could directly influence events on the battlefield.

and the Stafford Heights overlooking the river. It was a great achievement to get such a large army moving so fast; but once at the Rappahannock, the Union forces halted. The bridge had been destroyed, and Burnside's army had to wait a month for pontoon bridges to arrive.

Robert E. Lee's Confederate army took full advantage of the delay. On November 19 James Longstreet's corps of 41,000 men arrived on Marye's Heights, a ridge overlooking the city, and began digging in. Thomas "Stonewall" Jackson's corps of 39,000 began to arrive and were posted to Longstreet's right flank, extending the Confederate position 7 miles (11 km) south to Prospect Hill. Lee was assembling an army of 90,000 men entrenched on heights from which they could fire on almost every inch of ground between them and the river.

Not until December 11 was Burnside able to bridge the river. His forces built six pontoon bridges under fire from Confederates in the city. By nightfall Burnside's men were occupying Fredericksburg.

Union attack

On December 12 Edwin V. Sumner's Union Right Grand Division formed up among Fredericksburg's streets, while William B. Franklin's Left Grand Division marched downstream to cross opposite Jackson in preparation for an attack the following day.

On December 13 Franklin made an assault with the aim of trying to capture Prospect Hill. By 9:00 A.M., however, just two small divisions had advanced, only to be pinned down by Confederate fire from Marye's Heights. By the afternoon Franklin's troops were still halted at the foot of the ridge. A counterattack drove the Union troops back. Franklin's assault was all but over for no gain.

Attack on Marye's Heights

Burnside's second attack was toward Longstreet. From 12:00 P.M. brigade after brigade of Sumner's Grand Division advanced out of the city, trying to cover the 800 yards (730 m) of open ground to the Confederate guns on Marye's Heights positioned behind a stone wall. There were 14 successive charges, but no Union soldier got within 100 feet (30 m) of the wall. By evening 6,500 Union troops lay dead and dying. One Union soldier described it as "a great slaughter pen."

Burnside ordered renewed attacks on December 14, but was persuaded by his officers that they would be futile. The next day he ordered his troops back across the river. His losses were awful: more than 12,000 killed or wounded. Confederate losses were 4,700. The battle proved to be one of the South's most overwhelming victories. Once again the Union army's advance to Richmond had failed. The defeat lowered morale in the Army of the Potomac and throughout the North.

Battle Details

1. On December 11 Union forces built six pontoon bridges across the river under continuous fire from the last Confederates in Fredericksburg. Union forces occupied and looted the city on the 12th.
2. On December 13 in the Union assault on Prospect Hill only two small divisions attacked due to mismanagement. The Confederates pushed them back to the river.
3. At 12:00 P.M. the main Union assault on the Confederate forces entrenched on Marye's Heights began. It continued until dark with no effect. Burnside evacuated Fredericksburg and retreated across the river on December 15.

Gaines' Mill, Battle of

The Battle of Gaines' Mill, Virginia, was fought on June 27, 1862. It was the second and most decisive of the Seven Days' Battles, in which Robert E. Lee's Army of Northern Virginia turned back a Union attempt to capture Richmond.

When General Robert E. Lee took command of his forces outside the Confederate capital of Richmond in June 1862, his 70,000 men faced a Union army of more than 100,000 men under George B. McClellan. Lee's army, the Army of Northern Virginia, was camped just outside the capital. With characteristic audacity Lee began a series of attacks, now known as the Seven Days' Campaign (June 25–July 1).

Seven Days' Campaign

Read about the campaign on pages 81–82.

Attacks on the Union army

Lee planned to attack the right flank of McClellan's Army of the Potomac, which was separated from the rest of the Union army by the Chickahominy River. The first attempt, at Mechanicsville on June 26, was bungled by Lee's inexperienced subordinates, but the attack forced McClellan to withdraw from Richmond south to the James River. On June 27 the Union army's rear guard took up a strong position on high ground between Cold Harbor and Mr. Gaines' farm and mill, which gave the battle its name.

As at Mechanicsville, Lee had problems coordinating assaults, and several attempts to take the strong Union position failed. Nearing sunset, a bold frontal attack by Texans led by John Bell Hood succeeded in breaking through the Union position, and at nightfall the rear guard joined in the general Union withdrawal. At a cost of 8,750 casualties, Lee had earned his first battlefield victory of the war. The battle also cemented the reputation of Hood's Texas Brigade as an accomplished and successful unit.

Curriculum Context

If you are asked to describe Robert E. Lee's career during the the war, you could include his first victory.

Gettysburg, Battle of

General Robert E. Lee's Confederate Army of Northern Virginia fought General George G. Meade's Union Army of the Potomac at Gettysburg, Pennsylvania, on July 1–3, 1863. Lasting for three days, it was the largest battle of the Civil War.

On June 16, 1863, Robert E. Lee ordered the Army of Northern Virginia across the Potomac to begin its second invasion of the North. The plan was to march through Maryland and into Pennsylvania and win a decisive battle there, and perhaps even take Washington, D.C. Three Confederate army corps were involved: II Corps under Richard S. Ewell, I Corps under James Longstreet, and III Corps under Ambrose P. Hill. Together with J.E.B. Stuart's cavalry corps, Lee's army numbered about 75,000 men.

The battle begins

The encounter that developed into the largest battle of the Civil War began almost by chance. On June 29 one of A.P. Hill's divisions under Harry Heth went foraging toward Gettysburg, Pennsylvania. Early on July 1 it ran into a Union cavalry brigade from John Buford's 1st Cavalry Division, posted about 4 miles (6.5 km) west of the town across the Chambersburg Pike. Gettysburg was always a potential battleground. It was strategically important because it lay at the junction of roads running out to Washington and Baltimore to the south and east and to Harrisburg, the capital of Pennsylvania, to the north. Once Lee and the Union commander George G. Meade learned that their armies had met there, both generals quickly ordered their forces to concentrate on the town.

Lee's Confederates began arriving from the north and northwest, while Meade's lead corps began arriving from the south. By mid-morning A.P. Hill was

> ### Curriculum Context
>
> Gettysburg was not only the war's largest battle; it was also a significant turning point of the whole conflict.

reinforcing Heth, while John F. Reynolds, commander of the Union I Corps, established a defensive line across the Chambersburg Pike at McPherson's Ridge. Reynolds fell in action, and Abner Doubleday took over his corps command.

Fighting developed north of the town with the arrival of Oliver O. Howard's Union XI Corps in the afternoon. They were pushed back through the town by two divisions of Ewell's corps, led by Jubal A. Early and Robert E. Rodes. The retreating Union forces were on the verge of losing the battle, but were rallied south of the town on Cemetery Hill by the arrival of Winfield Scott Hancock and the lead unit of his II Corps. With the McPherson's Ridge position now outflanked, Doubleday also withdrew to Cemetery Hill. By the end

Curriculum Context

Some curricula ask students to understand how close the Union came to defeat at Gettysburg.

Battle Details

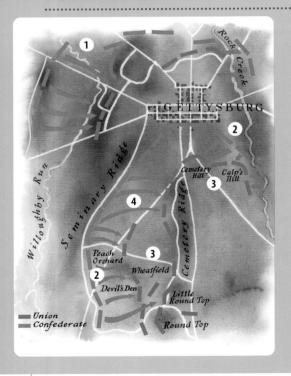

1. On July 1 the Confederates advanced from the north but were stopped as both sides sent troops forward quickly. The Confederates occupied Gettysburg, and Union forces fell back to the high ground to the south of the town.

2. On July 2 Union forces were pushed back as fierce fighting took place around the Devil's Den and Peach Orchard, but the Union line held.

3. In the late afternoon Confederates made piecemeal attacks on Cemetery Hill and Culp's Hill but made no headway.

4. On July 3, 15,000 Confederates made a doomed frontal assault, later known as Pickett's Charge. The failure of this attack marked the effective end of the battle.

of the first day the Confederates held the town but Union forces were secure on Cemetery Hill and also on Culp's Hill a little to the east. Both armies reinforced during the night.

The second day

By July 2 Meade had more than 90,000 men consolidating their position on the high ground, which extended in a fishhook-shaped line from Culp's Hill around Cemetery Hill and south along Cemetery Ridge. On the Confederate side Hill and Ewell had been joined by Longstreet, whom Lee ordered to take position along Seminary Ridge next to Hill's corps on the Confederate right. Lee planned to attack both Meade's flanks on the second day. Longstreet would begin the attack by a strike at the Union left.

The fighting began in the afternoon with a disaster for the Union. Daniel E. Sickles, leading III Corps, advanced without orders from Cemetery Ridge toward the Emmitsburg Road. Caught in open ground by Longstreet's troops, III Corps was cut to pieces in savage fighting around the Peach Orchard and Devil's Den. The Union left flank was now exposed, and a Confederate division under John Bell Hood advanced toward a hill position known as Little Round Top, which dominated the south of the Cemetery Ridge.

Fortunately for the Union forces, Gouverneur K. Warren had spotted the importance of Little Round Top and ordered troops to occupy it. Hood's attacks on the hill reached the lower slopes but failed to break through to the top. On the Confederate left attacks by Ewell's corps on Cemetery Hill and Culp's Hill did not begin until early evening and had made no gains by the time darkness fell. The Confederate flank attacks had been piecemeal and uncoordinated; both had failed. Meade still held his ground.

Flanks

The sides of a military formation.

Curriculum Context

At the time of the Civil War, armies did not have the technology to continue fighting during darkness.

A painting by Edwin Forbes of Union troops on the summit of Little Round Top in the early evening of July 3, 1863, the final day of the Battle of Gettysburg.

Pickett's Charge

This remarkable action is described in detail on page 76.

Curriculum Context

Many curricula expect students to appreciate Gettysburg's significance as the "high-water mark of the Confederacy"—the closest Southern forces came to the ultimate defeat of the North.

The third day

On the third day of battle, July 3, Lee made a final bid to break the Union center on Cemetery Ridge. He concentrated his artillery—some 150 guns—on Seminary Ridge and ordered three infantry divisions, totaling 15,000 men, to make a frontal assault across nearly a mile (1.6 km) of open ground toward the Union positions ranged above them behind a stone wall. At 1:00 P.M. the guns opened up and started the biggest Confederate artillery bombardment of the war. It lasted two hours during which the leading Confederate division commanded by George E. Pickett moved into position. At about 3:00 P.M. the guns fell silent, and Pickett began his famous charge.

Pickett's Charge

Union artillery opened up first, pouring shell, shot, and canister into the advancing ranks until the survivors were within 200 yards (180 m) of the Union front line. Then the infantry opened up with volley on volley of musket fire. Only a handful of men reached the stone wall. All Lee could say was, "It's all my fault. It is I who have lost this fight," admitting his gross tactical error.

On July 4 Lee ordered his defeated army back to Virginia. Confederate casualties numbered more than 20,000; the Union total was 23,000. The two armies left more than 6,000 dead on the field. The Confederacy never again threatened the Northern capital.

Grierson's Raid

Union Colonel Benjamin H. Grierson led the Civil War's most successful cavalry expedition. On April 17, 1863, he took three regiments deep into Mississippi to divert Confederate forces while Ulysses S. Grant moved on Vicksburg.

General Ulysses S. Grant planned for the cavalry raiders to divert Confederate forces protecting Vicksburg so he could move his army south of the strategically vital city on the Mississippi River.

On April 17, 1863, Grierson led the 2nd Iowa, 6th Illinois, and 7th Illinois cavalry out of La Grange, Tennessee, south into Mississippi. The Confederate cavalry tried to intercept them, but Grierson confused them repeatedly. Reports of Grierson's movements tricked General John C. Pemberton, commander of Confederate forces at Vicksburg, into moving troops away from the Mississippi River to trap the Union raiders. At one time 20,000 Confederate troops were committed to stopping Grierson—men who were therefore unable to oppose Grant's river crossing. Grierson's men also succeeded in doing much damage to bridges and railroads behind Vicksburg. They tore up the Southern Mississippi Railroad, the only rail link between the eastern and western parts of the Confederacy.

Escape to Baton Rouge

Southern troops never caught Grierson's raiders. After ravaging 600 miles (960 km) of Confederate territory, Grierson once more did the unexpected: He escaped back behind Union lines by riding south to Union-held Baton Rouge, Louisiana, rather than north.

Vicksburg
Read about Grant's campaign against Vicksburg on pages 96–97.

Grierson's route took him through the heart of the South.

Hampton Roads, Battle of

The Battle of Hampton Roads took place off Virginia on March 8–9, 1862. By demonstrating the superiority of ironclads over wooden ships, the battle changed naval history. It was also the first naval battle between armored ships.

Curriculum Context

If you are asked to give examples of technological innovation during the war, the ironclad is a rare example in which the South led the more industrialized North.

At the beginning of the Civil War the Union established a naval blockade of the Southern coastline. To counter the blockade, the Confederacy concentrated on building ironclads, a new type of armored ship that had never been used in combat.

The Confederates converted a partly destroyed Union ship they had captured, the *Merrimack*, into an ironclad, with 4 inches (10 cm) of iron armor plating and an iron ram mounted on its bow. Renamed the CSS *Virginia*, the vessel steamed out on a trial cruise from Norfolk, Virginia, into Hampton Roads on March 8, 1862.

After a successful trial, the commanding officer, Franklin Buchanan, decided to attack Union ships blockading Chesapeake Bay. In just a few hours the *Virginia* destroyed two large Union warships, USS *Cumberland* and USS *Congress*, and damaged USS *Minnesota*. The ironclad showed that the mainly wooden and sail-powered U.S. fleet was obsolete.

Curriculum Context

The success of the ironclads began a dash by navies around the world to construct iron rather than wooden vessels.

Draft

The depth of a boat that is under the water.

Duel of the ironclads

The next morning the *Virginia* returned to Hampton Roads to continue the battle. To the crew's great surprise, it was met by an enemy ironclad, the USS *Monitor*. Smaller than the *Virginia*, the *Monitor* featured a revolving gun turret, a shallower draft, and a higher top speed, which enabled it to outmaneuver the *Virginia* in the running battle that developed. The two vessels pounded each other for almost four hours at close range, eventually fighting to a standstill. At nightfall the *Virginia* withdrew into the James River. It had been hit 97 times over the two days, and the *Monitor* 21 times, but neither was badly damaged. Two months later the *Virginia* was sunk by its crew to prevent it falling into Union hands—the ironclad had been trapped in the Norfolk shipyard when the Union retook the city.

By fending off the *Virginia*, the *Monitor* preserved the Union blockade. Although the Battle of Hampton Roads was a minor battle in terms of immediate impact, it led to a change in naval warfare. Both sides, realizing the impact the ironclads had made, accelerated their ironclad-building programs. The Confederacy was never able to match the Union's ironclad production, however, and suffered naval defeat as a result.

The Confederate ironclad CSS *Virginia* (right) exchanges fire with Union ironclad USS *Monitor* during the Battle of Hampton Roads, Virginia, in March 1862.

Henry and Donelson, Forts

The capture of Forts Henry and Donelson in February 1862 was the first major Union victory of the war. It cost the Confederacy control over two critical rivers and signaled the emergence of the North's greatest general, Ulysses S. Grant.

Constructed in the fall of 1861, the forts were part of a Confederate defensive line that stretched across Kentucky from Columbus on the Mississippi River to Mill Springs in the Appalachian foothills. Fort Henry guarded the Tennessee River, and Fort Donelson the nearby Cumberland River. The waterways crossed the Kentucky–Tennessee border 65 miles (105 km) northwest of Nashville.

Curriculum Context

Ulysses S. Grant features in some curricula as an example of an individual who influenced the course of the war.

Union commanders realized that gaining control of the forts would give access to a huge area. Accordingly, Ulysses S. Grant was ordered to seize Fort Henry. On February 2, 1862, he steamed up the Ohio and Tennessee rivers with 17,000 men. Two days later his troops began to disembark 3 miles (5 km) from the fort, though a shortage of transports meant that it took more than a day to get the entire force into position. Meanwhile, Union ironclad gunboats under Andrew H. Foote conducted a bombardment of the fort. The fort was not in good shape to fend off this attack. It was poorly sited, unfinished, and half-flooded. Realizing that an all-out defense of the fort was pointless, Confederate commander Lloyd Tilghman sent most of his 3,000-man force to Fort Donelson. He remained at Fort Henry with an 80-man artillery battery to conduct a delaying action.

Strike Colors

To lower one's flag as an indication of surrender.

Fort Henry surrenders

On February 6, as Grant's infantrymen made their way toward the fort, Foote's gunboats renewed the attack. Tilghman struck his colors, and Foote accepted his

surrender. The Tennessee River was suddenly a Union highway as far south as Muscle Shoals, Alabama. The loss of Fort Henry unhinged the Confederacy's western line. The overall Southern commander, Albert S. Johnston, evacuated his forces from Columbus and Bowling Green, Kentucky. He also reinforced the garrison at Fort Donelson so that within days 21,000 troops occupied the fort and its earthworks.

Bad weather delayed the Union advance, but on February 12 Grant's forces marched from Fort Henry toward Fort Donelson, which they surrounded two days later. Foote's gunboats bombarded the fort on February 14, but suffered severe damage in return from its well-sited cannons. Grant then decided to wait for reinforcements to arrive before making a major attempt to take the fort.

Union gunboats commanded by Andrew H. Foote bombard Fort Henry from the Tennessee River, February 6, 1862. Confederate forces surrendered the fort on the same day.

Bombard

To subject to a sustained artillery attack.

Attack on Fort Donelson

Confederate leadership was poor. The fort's commander, John B. Floyd, vetoed a breakout from the fort at a time when most of the garrison could have easily escaped. Then, when a surprise attack on February 15 punched a hole in the Union line, his second-in-command, Gideon J. Pillow, threw away the chance to escape by trying to destroy Grant's army. Pillow's action gave Grant time to order counterattacks that forced the Confederates back into the fort.

On the night of February 16 the fort's commanders decided to surrender. Floyd feared that, since he had been the U.S. secretary of war until 1860, the Union government might try him for treason. He therefore resolved to join part of the garrison that planned to escape from the fort under cover of night. He turned command over to Pillow, who immediately passed it to his subordinate, the fort's third-ranking officer, Simon Bolivar Buckner.

Floyd, Pillow, and about 5,000 Confederate troops fled. The next morning Buckner sent a message to Grant, an old West Point classmate, asking for surrender terms. In words that soon electrified the North, Grant replied, "No terms except unconditional and immediate surrender can be accepted." About 15,000 Southerners capitulated. Between 1,500 and 3,500 Confederates had been killed or wounded in the earlier battles. Of a total force of 27,000 men Union casualties were 500 killed, 2,100 wounded, and 220 missing.

Treason

A crime against the government of one's own country.

Unconditional surrender

A surrender where terms are dictated by the victors and are not subject to negotiation.

Jonesboro, Battle of

The Battle of Jonesboro was the last battle in Union General William T. Sherman's campaign to capture Atlanta, Georgia. On August 31 and September 1, 1864, Sherman's forces fought John Bell Hood's Confederate Army of Tennessee.

At the end of July 1864 John Bell Hood's Confederate army in Atlanta was being bombarded by Union General William T. Sherman's forces. On August 25 Sherman withdrew most of his army to cut the railroads west and south of Atlanta. By cutting the Confederates' supply line, they would be forced out of the city. Hood, however, interpreted Sherman's movements as a retreat. When he received reports of Union troops near Jonesboro, he sent troops under William J. Hardee to destroy them. Hood's failure to perceive the danger facing him had dire consequences.

On August 31 Hardee was surprised to encounter not raiders but almost the entire Union force. His attack failed, and the Confederates suffered high casualties. This failure forced other Confederate corps back to a defensive position along the Macon and Western Railroad. On September 1 Sherman cut the railroad north of Jonesboro, attacking again in the afternoon to force a Confederate retreat. With the last supply line cut, Hood had to evacuate Atlanta. Union troops entered the city the next day on September 2.

Confederate defeat

The Battle of Jonesboro and the loss of Atlanta removed any doubt the Confederacy would lose the war. Sherman's forces suffered 1,150 casualties, and a total of 35,000 for the whole Atlanta campaign, but gave Lincoln the victory he needed. The mismanaged attacks at Jonesboro showed the command failures that plagued the Confederate Army of Tennessee.

Atlanta

The fall of Atlanta is described on pages 16–18.

Curriculum Context

You may be asked to give examples of poor military organization on the battlefield.

Kennesaw Mountain, Battle of

After a month of maneuvering through Georgia, Confederate General Joseph E. Johnston's army made a stand at Kennesaw Mountain near Marietta, Georgia, where it was attacked by William T. Sherman's Union troops on June 27, 1864.

On May 5, 1864, Sherman and his three Union armies of nearly 100,000 men, began to move south out of Tennessee toward Atlanta, Georgia. Johnston's 60,000 Confederate troops tried to block the advance. The campaign became one of maneuver. For a month the two forces moved deeper into Georgia. Sherman avoided committing his troops to a full attack by using his superior numbers to push Johnston back. By mid-June Johnston's troops were backed against a ridgeline anchored by Kennesaw Mountain, Georgia. Believing the line stretched, Sherman decided to attack.

Union attack

At dawn on June 27 Union forces advanced toward the well-entrenched Confederates. Diversionary attacks against the Confederate flanks had little effect. An assault against Pigeon Hill, south of Kennesaw Mountain, was met by deadly fire, forcing the attackers to withdraw. The main assault occurred just south of Pigeon Hill, where 8,000 Union troops were ordered to advance using only fixed bayonets. The advance soon degenerated into confusion as men were halted by concentrated fire from the earthworks to their front. By noon Sherman's men could take no more. The battle had proved to be a disaster. Union casualties for the day totaled 3,000; Confederate losses were 552. After the battle Sherman decided to return to his strategy of maneuver, flanking Johnston to the west and racing for the Chattahoochie River and Atlanta. Johnston had no choice but to move south, hoping once again to entice Sherman into battle on ground favorable to defense.

Diversionary

Actions intended to divert the enemy from a major military action.

Curriculum Context

The inability of a massed bayonet charge to defeat well-entrenched defenders armed with firearms was one sign of how the nature of modern warfare was changing during the Civil War.

March to the Sea and the Carolinas Campaign

In late 1864 Union General William T. Sherman led his troops on a destructive march through Georgia to the sea and then north through the Carolinas. This demonstration of strength was one of the most famous episodes of the war.

Following his capture of Atlanta, Georgia, on September 3, 1864, Union General William T. Sherman rested his army and planned his next move. His supply line, the railroad from Chattanooga, Tennessee, was under constant attack by the Confederate Army of Tennessee. After several weeks trying to protect the railroad, Sherman realized it was an impossible task. He decided instead to march to Savannah, a port on the Atlantic Coast 220 miles (350 km) away. On the march his men would live off the land.

The capture of Savannah would enable Union ships to supply the army and give Sherman a secure base from which to operate. Sherman also hoped that the march would strike a psychological blow to the Confederacy. He wrote of the plan to Ulysses S. Grant, "If we can march a well-appointed army right through [Confederate] territory, it is a demonstration ... that we have a power which [Jefferson] Davis cannot resist." On the way his troops would cut supply lines and "smash things generally." Sherman was an advocate of total war. He argued that to win, the Union had to break the South's will to resist by making "old and young, rich and poor, feel the hard hand of war."

A daring plan

Abandoning the supply line was risky, but Sherman was confident that Georgia farms produced more than enough to feed his troops. There was also a second risk.

> **Curriculum Context**
>
> Students might be asked to explain why Sherman's march through the South was so controversial.

> **Curriculum Context**
>
> Was Sherman right to insist that civilians should be made to feel the hardships of the war? What might have been his objective?

Between November 15, 1864, and March 25, 1865, Union troops marched 600 miles (960 km) through Georgia and the Carolinas. The marches showed how weak the Confederacy had become, and their destructiveness demoralized the Southern people.

Sherman intended to turn away from the Confederate Army of Tennessee, leaving it free to try to invade Union-occupied Tennessee. To counter this threat, Sherman sent 35,000 troops back to defend Nashville in November 1864. Then he burned everything of military value in Atlanta—about one-third of the city accidentally burned as well—and on November 15 set out with 60,000 men to Savannah.

Unopposed march

As Sherman's men headed southeast, the Confederates turned back to Tennessee as predicted to embark on an ill-fated invasion. This left no forces to oppose Sherman except Confederate cavalry and Georgia militia. As a result, Sherman was able to spread his army along a path 60 miles (95 km) wide. By moving in such a dispersed pattern, his army greatly eased the task of supplying itself from the countryside. Parties of foragers set out each day to scour the land for pork,

Foragers

Groups who collected food and other supplies, but did not pay for them.

beef, corn, and other foods. As the troops advanced, they paused regularly to wreck railroads and burn factories, cotton gins, and anything else that might be valuable to the Confederate war effort. In many cases the authorized foraging was accompanied by theft and vandalism, officially deplored but unofficially tolerated. There were also thousands of lawless stragglers following the army, who were beyond military control. Even some of Sherman's battle-hardened men voiced misgivings about the harsh treatment of civilians.

Curriculum Context

Could military commanders be held responsible for the actions of people outside their control?

Some of the most badly treated Southerners were the African American slaves liberated by the Union army. On one occasion a Union general burned a bridge over a creek to prevent any African Americans from following. He did so knowing that the Confederate cavalry was just a short distance away. Hundreds of slaves found their path to freedom blocked, and some drowned trying to swim the stream and escape.

Curriculum Context

If you are asked to describe the experiences of freed slaves in the war, you should remember that some were badly treated by Union soldiers.

Sherman captured Savannah on December 21, 1864. His next move was to join forces with Ulysses S. Grant in Virginia and defeat Robert E. Lee's army on the Richmond–Petersburg front. Sherman considered moving his troops by sea from Savannah but then determined on a second march through the Carolinas. The march began on February 1, 1865.

Sherman in the Carolinas

This march was more challenging than the first. There were more Confederate troops obstructing Sherman's advance, as well as several swampy rivers. Winter rains had turned the roads to mud. Nevertheless the Union troops surprised the Confederate command with the speed of their advance.

The destruction in South Carolina was much more widespread than in Georgia. This time the targets for pillaging and burning included towns and homes.

Pillage

To loot and plunder

Curriculum Context

Was it fair that Union soldiers blamed South Carolina for inciting the war?

South Carolina had been the first state to secede and was seen by many Union soldiers as responsible for the war. For this, Sherman wrote, "the whole army is burning with an insatiable desire to wreak vengeance on South Carolina." The worst single event was the burning of Columbia, the state capital, on February 17–18, 1865, although whether it was Union troops or retreating Confederates who started the fire remains a matter of controversy.

By early March Sherman's army had crossed into North Carolina. Joseph E. Johnston's Confederates tried to stop its progress at Bentonville on March 19–21, but failed. A few days later Sherman occupied Raleigh, the state capital.

Within weeks the war was over. Johnston surrendered to Sherman on April 26. Sherman's marches through Georgia and the Carolinas had been decisive. They showed how weak the Confederacy had become, while their destructiveness demoralized the population and hastened its defeat.

Sherman's Troops in Columbia

Emma LeConte was a young girl living in Columbia, South Carolina, when Sherman's troops occupied the city on February 17–18, 1865. She describes her experience:

"At about seven o'clock ... Henry told me there was a fire on Main Street. Sumter Street was brightly lighted by a burning house so near our piazza that we could feel the heat. By the red glare we could watch the wretches walking—generally staggering—back and forth from the camp to the town—shouting—hurrahing—cursing South Carolina—swearing—blaspheming—singing ribald songs and using obscene language.... The drunken devils roamed about setting fire to every house the flames seemed likely to spare ... They would enter houses and in the presence of helpless women and children, pour turpentine on the beds and set them on fire.... The wind blew a fearful gale, wafting the flames from house to house with frightful rapidity. By midnight the town (except the outskirts) was wrapped in one huge blaze."

Mobile Bay, Battle of

After capturing New Orleans and gaining control of the Mississippi River, the Union targeted Mobile Bay. On the morning of August 5, 1864, Union naval forces under David G. Farragut sailed into the bay and began to attack.

The main entrance to Mobile Bay was defended by Fort Morgan with 40 guns and Fort Gaines with 16 guns; sea mines (then known as torpedoes) were placed along the channel. Confederate forces under Franklin Buchanan consisted of the powerful ironclad CSS *Tennessee*, three wooden ships, 427 men, and 22 guns. David G. Farragut led a Union fleet of 14 wooden ships, four ironclad monitors, 2,700 men, and 197 guns.

"Go Ahead!"

The Union ironclad USS *Tecumseh* fired the first shot as the Union fleet entered the channel on August 5. Wooden ships were fastened together in pairs to face the heavy fire from Fort Morgan. The *Tecumseh* hit a mine and sank quickly. At its sinking, the captain of the leading ship, the USS *Brooklyn*, halted in confusion and signaled for advice from Farragut.

From his flagship, the USS *Hartford*, Farragut issued his famous rallying order: "Damn the torpedoes! Go ahead!" The *Hartford* then led the rest of the Union fleet into the bay without losing another vessel. They soon overwhelmed the three wooden Confederate ships. For almost two hours the *Tennessee* continued the fight alone against the entire Union fleet. Its 6-inch-thick (15-cm) iron armor was pounded with solid shot. At least three Union ships repeatedly rammed the *Tennessee* at full speed. Surrounded by enemy ships, the badly damaged *Tennessee* surrendered. The three-hour battle ended in a Union victory. Each side lost 300 men killed, wounded or captured. The city of Mobile

> **Ironclad**
> A new type of warship that was protected by an outer skin of iron armor.

> **Curriculum Context**
> David G. Farragut was the outstanding Union naval commander of the war.

Outnumbered by 17 to 1, the Confederate ironclad CSS *Tennessee* (center) continued the Battle of Mobile Bay alone after the other Confederate ships were overwhelmed. After nearly two hours the ironclad finally surrendered.

remained in Confederate hands for eight months, but the Union had achieved its goal of closing the port and completing the blockade of supplies to the South.

By the third week in August Union troops had succeeded in capturing Fort Powell, which guarded Grant's Pass into Mobile Bay, and Forts Morgan and Gaines at the bay's main entrance. The Union victory at Mobile Bay, along with the capture of Atlanta, Georgia on September 2, boosted Northern morale and President Lincoln's chances of reelection in November.

Murfreesboro (Stone's River), Batttle of

This hard-fought battle was waged in central Tennessee on December 31, 1862, and January 2, 1863, between the Union Army of the Cumberland under William S. Rosecrans and Braxton Bragg's Confederate Army of Tennessee.

In December 1862 Rosecrans ordered his army south to Murfreesboro, where Bragg's troops were assembled. On December 30 the two armies met near Stone's River. The Confederates struck at dawn next day, enjoying early success as seven brigades fell on two brigades guarding the Union flank. But the attack did not lead to a rout; the Union army conducted a fighting retreat.

The Army of Tennessee repeatedly assaulted the Union forces, while Rosecrans tried to hold his ground. By nightfall, the Confederates had driven their opponents back more than 2 miles (3.2 km). Bragg wired Richmond that the Union army was in retreat. To his surprise, however, dawn revealed the Union army still in place. Fighting resumed on January 2, when Bragg ordered a frontal assault on an isolated Union position. Initial success turned into a Union repulse of the Confederates. Bragg ordered a retreat on the morning of January 3, his decision swayed by the false impression that the Union had been reinforced.

Many casualties

The battle was one of the hardest fought of the war. Of Bragg's 35,000 troops, around 9,450 were casualties. The Union forces lost some 9,500 of their 41,400 men. The battle was a strategic victory for the Union , which secured control of Kentucky and increased its hold on Tennessee. Lincoln telegraphed his battered but unyielding troops a heartfelt "God bless you."

Rout

An indisciplined and panicked retreat as soldiers flee for their lives.

Curriculum Context

The use of the telegraph by both sides at Murfreesboro is an example of the impact of technological change on the nature of the war.

Nashville, Battle of

Fought between John Bell Hood's Confederate Army of Tennessee and the Union Army of the Cumberland on December 15–16, 1864, the battle at Nashville, Tennessee, was the culmination of the last Confederate offensive in the West.

Sherman

Read about the destructiveness of Sherman's campaign on pages 63–66.

Franklin

The Battle of Franklin is described on page 46.

Curriculum Context

Why might Grant have been reluctant for Thomas to become besieged in Nashville?

In late November Confederate General John Bell Hood led 30,000 men of the Army of Tennessee north out of Alabama. His objective was to recapture Tennessee and to put pressure on Union General William T. Sherman to call a halt to his highly destructive and demoralizing campaign through Georgia.

By the end of the month Hood had advanced his army north through Pulaski and Columbia, and had turned back a Union force of 27,000 outside Franklin. This battle cost Hood's army more than 6,200 casualties, including six generals, but Hood did not stop. On December 2 the Confederates were south of Nashville facing the strong Union fortifications that ringed the city. With winter coming on, Hood ordered his men to dig in for a siege.

On December 6, inside Nashville, George H. Thomas, the commander of the Union Army of the Cumberland, received orders from Ulysses S. Grant not to wait out a siege but to attack Hood at once. Thomas, however, was still planning his strategy and did not launch his attack until the early morning of December 15.

Before daylight Thomas's men struck Hood's right flank, where they pinned down three Confederate divisions. At noon 35,000 Union troops attacked the Confederate left, forcing Hood to withdraw his line a mile (1.5 km) to the south. Hood's new position was a strong one, protected by Peach Tree Hill on the right and Shy's Hill on the left.

A decisive victory

On December 16, despite rain and sleet, Thomas attacked again. The Confederate right was hit first but managed to hold. On the left, Union forces took Shy's Hill, and Union cavalry gained the Confederate rear. Then another attack came in on Hood's center, and his whole line gave way.

The Army of Tennessee was routed. It now numbered barely 17,000 men and in the course of its defeat it had lost most of its equipment. Hood retreated to Tupelo, Mississippi, and in January resigned his command. In contrast, Thomas was promoted to major general and was voted the thanks of Congress.

General Hood's Confederate troops camped around Nashville in December 1864. Despite devastating losses at the Battle of Franklin two weeks earlier, Hood still hoped to drive the Union forces out of Tennessee.

Peninsular Campaign

In March 1862 the Union launched a major campaign to capture the Confederate capital of Richmond, Virginia. Led by General George B. McClellan, Union forces landed on the Virginia peninsula, planning to attack Richmond from the east.

Curriculum Context

Students might be expected to describe the advantages of the North's naval superiority.

President Lincoln wanted an offensive straight through northern Virginia, but the commander of the Army of the Potomac, George B. McClellan, suggested instead exploiting the Union navy's control of the coast by transporting troops from the Potomac River down Chesapeake Bay to the Union-held Fort Monroe. The Union army would then be only 75 miles (120 km) from Richmond, and could be kept supplied by sea.

Lincoln reluctantly agreed to the plan, but was worried that Washington would be left undefended. By the end of March Confederate General "Stonewall" Jackson was active in the Shenandoah Valley, which also alarmed the Union authorities. Although McClellan intended to leave enough troops to defend the capital, Lincoln withdrew a whole corps from McClellan's command to remain in northern Virginia. This was the start of a breakdown in the relationship between McClellan and Lincoln's government that adversely affected the Peninsular Campaign.

Army on the move

By April 1 McClellan had more than 60,000 men and 100 guns at Fort Monroe, with another 40,000 men on the way. The Confederates reacted quickly. General John B. Magruder, who was responsible for the defense of the peninsula, hastily built two defensive lines between the York and James Rivers, and fooled McClellan into believing that his tiny force of 13,000 was much larger by carrying out a series of deceptive maneuvers. Faced with the Yorktown defenses,

Curriculum Context

During the Peninsular Campaign, Confederate defensive lines made good use of the rivers in the region.

McClellan stalled his advance. He was convinced he faced a Confederate army of at least 100,000; and he laid siege to Yorktown. Despite Lincoln's telegrams urging him to advance, McClellan spent a month besieging Yorktown, giving Confederate General Joseph E. Johnston the chance to come south with his army and reinforce Magruder. There were now 75,000 Confederates on the south bank of the Chickahominy River a few miles east of Richmond. Johnston took command of Confederate forces and ordered Magruder to evacuate Yorktown. Magruder retreated on May 4, and McClellan began to advance, taking Williamsburg on May 5 as Johnston pulled his forces back.

By the end of May the armies faced one another around the villages of Fair Oaks and Seven Pines near the flooding Chickahominy, which would play a vital part in the coming battles. McClellan divided his army, concentrating 60,000 men on the north side of the river and leaving 31,500 on the south side. Communications between the two wings of the army were poor because there were few bridges.

Curriculum Context

Lincoln became convinced that McClellan was not aggressive enough, and began to consider replacing him.

Campaign Details

The Union Army of the Potomac led by George B. McClellan landed on the Virginia peninsula at Fort Monroe. McClellan besieged Yorktown for a month from early April, then took Williamsburg on May 5. The Confederates attacked at Fair Oaks on May 31 and June 1, but the Union army held its ground. After the Seven Days' Battles, fought on the outskirts of Richmond between June 25 and July 1, the Union army was forced to retreat to Harrison's Landing on the James River, ending the Union's Peninsular Campaign.

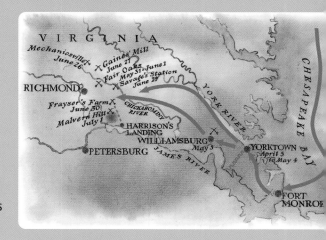

Fair Oaks

There's more about the Battle of Fair Oaks (Seven Pines) on page 43.

Battle of Fair Oaks (Seven Pines)

On May 31 Johnston launched an attack on McClellan's southern wing. The attack was poorly executed, and by the end of the day the Union forces still held the ground, despite losing 5,050 men. The Confederates suffered 6,150 casualties, including Johnston, who was so badly wounded that on June 1 General Robert E. Lee took command of the Confederate army. Lee ordered an immediate withdrawal. For the next two weeks, in torrential rain, both sides consolidated their positions. Lee ordered his new command, which he named the Army of Northern Virginia, to strengthen Richmond's defenses as he planned his first offensive. McClellan meanwhile was preparing to attack Richmond with heavy artillery, once again relying on siege tactics.

Seven Days' Campaign

Find out about the Seven Days' Campaign on pages 81–82.

The Seven Days' Campaign

On June 12 Lee sent cavalry commander J.E.B. Stuart and 1,200 men to find McClellan's exact location. Stuart was back in Richmond on June 15. He reported that McClellan had moved four corps south of the Chickahominy, leaving only one corps on the north bank near Mechanicsville, protecting the Union supply base at White House Landing on the Pamunkey River. This corps and supply base were the target of Lee's first attack. The Battle of Mechanicsville on June 26 was the first of the Seven Days' Campaign. Union forces were pushed back but held onto a position north of the Chickahominy, only to be attacked again on the 27th at Gaines' Mill, forcing their withdrawal south of the river.

Curriculum Context

The Peninsular Campaign marked the emergence of Robert E. Lee, who would become the South's most aggressive and successful commander.

Union withdrawal

McClellan, with his left flank under pressure from Lee, abandoned White House. On the 27th he ordered his forces south toward the James River. The battles of the Seven Days' Campaign were now Union rearguard actions to frustrate Lee's attempts to deliver a killer blow. By July 2 McClellan's army was back at Harrison's Landing: the Peninsular Campaign had failed.

Petersburg, Siege of

For 10 months, between June 1864 and March 1865, General Robert E. Lee's Confederate Army of Northern Virginia was besieged at the city of Petersburg, Virginia, by General Ulysses S. Grant's Union Army of the Potomac.

On June 15, 1864, Grant sent 100,000 men of the Army of the Potomac south from Cold Harbor across the James River to swing west through Petersburg and attack Lee from the rear. Union forces were stopped at Petersburg by a Confederate force hastily organized by General P.G.T. Beauregard. Two days later Lee ordered most of his army south to reinforce Petersburg, a vital rail center. Confederate forces set up fortifications southeast of the city that could not be breached by frontal assault. Instead, Grant kept his army attacking to the west and south. His objectives were the two railroads that supplied Lee's army and the Appomattox River, which marked Lee's line of retreat to the west.

Curriculum Context

Students might be asked to explain the significance of the railroad network to the course of the war.

In late August Union forces cut the railroad running south. Grant attacked again in late September and late October, extending the siege lines to 35 miles (55 km) and threatening the last rail line open to Lee. Lee's position was desperate. Heavily outnumbered, he did not have enough troops to man all the fortifications.

Trench warfare

During the winter the siege degenerated into grim trench warfare. This stalemate continued until February 1865, when Grant renewed his attacks. On March 29 Grant began his final push, sending 125,000 men to flank Lee's trench line. At the Battle of Five Forks on April 1 they overwhelmed a Confederate force of 10,000 and threatened to cut off Lee's line of retreat. Lee pulled out of Petersburg on April 2, retreating westward. It was the beginning of the end for his army.

Five Forks

The battle is described on pages 44–45.

Pickett's Charge

On the last day of the Battle of Gettysburg 15,000 Confederates made a doomed assault to try to capture the high ground. It became known as Pickett's Charge after George E. Pickett, the commander of the charge's leading division.

Curriculum Context

You might be asked to explain why the furthest advance of Pickett's Charge—one of the war's most famous actions—is sometimes referred to as "the high-water mark of the Confederacy."

On July 3, 1863, the third day of Gettysburg, General Robert E. Lee ordered a frontal assault on the Union position along Cemetery Ridge. George E. Pickett's division spearheaded the attack. With just under 15,000 Confederate troops, Pickett would try to break the Union hold on the ridge, which lay a mile (1.6 km) from Southern lines. Lee brought all his 150 guns to his position on Seminary Ridge. At 1:00 P.M. they opened fire and began a two-hour bombardment of the Union line. At 3:00 P.M. the guns fell silent. The Confederates moved over the open land. But the bombardment had not done its job. Union infantry waited behind a stone wall, and the artillery was waiting behind the ridge.

Terrible carnage

As the Confederates marched up, 80 Union guns opened fire, causing terrible carnage. Through this onslaught the Confederates kept coming, aiming for a position on the ridge now known as the Copse of Trees. Holding it were the 69th and 71st Pennsylvania Infantry. Confederate troops were within 200 yards (180 m) of the wall when the Union troops opened fire, mowing down the attackers. Barely 100 Southerners reached the wall before the attack finally halted.

A painting by Edwin Forbes of Confederate troops advancing across open ground toward the Union forces on Cemetery Ridge at Gettysburg on July 3, 1863, in the attack known as Pickett's Charge.

Port Hudson, Siege of

A small town just north of Baton Rouge, Louisiana, Port Hudson was one of the most heavily fortified Confederate positions on the Mississippi River. After the fall of New Orleans in April 1862 it became a target of Union offensives.

Port Hudson was the next step in a progressive Union attempt to move upriver in the direction of Vicksburg, Mississippi. As General Ulysses S. Grant continued his efforts to capture Vicksburg in early 1863, General Nathaniel P. Banks formed a plan to move against Port Hudson. Confederate General Franklin Gardner had received reinforcements and turned the town into a system of fortified positions facing out over the river toward the landward approaches.

A naval attack

The first attempt to capture Port Hudson was a gunboat attack under David G. Farragut, but it failed. On May 11, 1863, land and naval forces under Banks moved out of Baton Rouge in a more concerted attack. Gardner had only 3,500 men against more than 30,000 Union troops, but he used them skillfully, and for two weeks held off a series of assaults, some of them by African American units recruited in New Orleans.

The failure of these attacks convinced Banks to settle into a siege in late May. Gardner had no hope of victory at this point; Confederate forces in Vicksburg were under siege, so there was no prospect of help. Supplies gradually ran out, while Banks's army remained well-supplied. When word reached Gardner that Vicksburg had surrendered on July 4, he too surrendered. The defense failed, but Gardner had succeeded in tying down over 30,000 Union troops. The Union victories at Port Hudson and Vicksburg secured Union control of the Mississippi River for the remainder of the war.

Curriculum Context

Sieges were a standard tactic of warfare in the 18th and 19th centuries; the attackers surrounded a city with defenses and starved the occupants into surrender.

Red River Campaign

When General Ulysses S. Grant took command of the Union armies in early 1864, he planned a series of offensives, one of which, under General Nathaniel P. Banks, would move from New Orleans, Louisiana, against the port of Mobile in Alabama.

Banks did not intend to head to Mobile. Instead, he envisioned an army and navy force, with troops and gunboats under David D. Porter, moving up the Red River to cooperate with another Union force under General Frederick Steele in capturing Shreveport, Louisiana, a major supply depot and gateway to Texas. Banks hoped to capture supplies of cotton as well.

Slow-moving transports

Banks and Porter left St. Martinville, Louisiana, on March 12. Porter's gunboats moved quickly and on March 16 took Alexandria, Louisiana. It took Banks' slow-moving transports carrying the troops almost two weeks to catch up. As Porter moved upriver to Shreveport, Banks marched his men along the west side of the Red River. On April 8 a Confederate force trapped and defeated Banks at Mansfield. Steele failed to support him as planned. Banks decided to retreat to New Orleans and Porter's flotilla was stranded by falling river levels. Only the construction of river dams near Alexandria by 3,000 troops rescued the boats and allowed them to escape. The Red River Campaign was a total fiasco that ended in complete failure.

Flotilla
A small naval unit of one or two squadrons of warships.

Union gunboats navigate through one of the dams built by Union soldiers at Alexandria, Louisiana. The dam raised the water level so the trapped vessels could escape as Confederate forces approached in May 1864.

Richmond, Fall of

By early 1865 General Robert E. Lee's Army of Northern Virginia was under siege at Petersburg, south of Richmond. Only Lee's fortifications were holding off the Union forces and keeping Richmond from falling into Union hands.

Union General Ulysses S. Grant's priority was the destruction of Lee's army. Once that went, he knew the rest of the Confederacy must fall. On March 29 Grant began a push to break the siege. With his forces barely 20 miles (32 km) from the Appomattox River, Grant sent troops west of Lee's thinly held lines. Led by Philip H. Sheridan, the force crushed 10,000 Confederates at the Battle of Five Forks on April 1. The next day Grant began a massive assault on Confederate defenses. Lee sent a telegram to Confederate President Jefferson Davis advising him that Petersburg was about to fall and that he should prepare to evacuate Richmond. Lee ordered all army units to retreat along the Appomattox.

Escape by train

On April 2 the Confederate government prepared to escape by train south to Danville, Virginia, hoping to meet up with the army and continue the war. Their train left at about 11:00 P.M. Meanwhile Richmond descended into chaos. Fires deliberately set in government buildings soon got out of control and destroyed much of the city. Looting was widespread. Early on April 3 Union cavalry raced into Richmond and raised the first U.S. flag over the former Confederate capitol building. They were followed by black troops of General Weitzel's corps. Weitzel took the city's official surrender and ordered his men to restore order and extinguish the fires. About 8:15 A.M. Grant received a telegram from Weitzel saying that Richmond was under Union control. Order was sufficiently restored for President Lincoln to make a personal visit on April 4.

> **Curriculum Context**
>
> Was it realistic to still hope to continue the war after the Confederate capital had fallen?

Savannah, Fall of

Savannah was the largest city in Georgia and a major port. It was a Confederate stronghold until late 1864, when it fell to Union General William T. Sherman at the end of his celebrated March to the Sea.

Strategic
Important as part of an overall military plan.

Savannah was well defended: with strong fortifications on all sides, the surrounding network of swamps and rivers formed a natural barrier. Its strategic importance was huge. Capturing the city would give Union General William T. Sherman a secure base inside Confederate territory and a port for his army's supplies.

At the start of December 1864 the city was garrisoned by 10,000 regular Confederate troops led by William J. Hardee. On December 9 and 10 Sherman's men surrounded all sides of the city apart from the seaboard flank. Despite their numerical superiority—there were 62,000—Sherman delayed his attack until he received badly needed supplies from the Union fleet. As he waited, one of his divisions assaulted and captured the Confederate Fort McAllister on the Ogeechee River south of Savannah. On December 16, Union ships steamed up the Ogeechee and delivered food, siege guns, and other equipment to the waiting army.

Ultimatum
A final demand, which if not met will result in violence.

Surrender or else

The next day, Sherman issued an ultimatum to Hardee. When Hardee refused to surrender, Sherman ordered John G. Foster, commander of Union forces in South Carolina, to seal off eastern approaches, the only escape route from the city. But before he did this, on the night of December 20, Hardee's men escaped across a hastily constructed pontoon bridge and disappeared into South Carolina. The next morning Union troops entered Savannah unopposed, bringing the March to the Sea to a triumphant conclusion.

Seven Days' Campaign

The Seven Days' Battles, fought near Richmond, Virginia, between June 26 and July 1, 1862, were the final engagements of Union General George B. McClellan's Peninsular Campaign and the first of the Confederate Army of Northern Virginia.

The Seven Days' Battles ended the attempt of the Army of the Potomac, led by George B. McClellan, to capture Richmond, the Confederate capital, in the Peninsular Campaign of spring 1862. McClellan's army of more than 100,000 men landed on the peninsula in March. By the end of May it was at Seven Pines, only 10 miles (16 km) from Richmond. Joseph E. Johnston's Confederate army attacked on May 31, but failed to dislodge the enemy. Johnston was wounded in the battle and was replaced by Robert E. Lee on June 1.

McClellan prepared to lay siege to Richmond, while Lee strengthened the city's defenses and planned an attack. A reconnaissance by J.E.B. Stuart's cavalry revealed that McClellan had divided his army on either side of the Chickahominy River. Lee targeted the one corps left on the north bank near Mechanicsville. Lee ordered "Stonewall" Jackson's army to join him from the Shenandoah Valley, which would give him 87,000 men.

McClellan changes plans

The Battle of Mechanicsville on June 26 was the first of the Seven Days' Campaign. Lee ordered 60,000 men across the Chickahominy against the Union right, which fell back. Despite initial success, the Confederate advance was uncoordinated; and a planned flanking maneuver on the Union right, which could have won the battle, failed because Jackson arrived too late.

The Union army held a line at Beaver Dam Creek, but McClellan ordered a withdrawal to Gaines' Mill, which

> ### Peninsular Campaign
> The campaign on the Virginia peninsula is described on pages 72–74.

Lee attacked on the 27th, forcing the Union army south across the Chickahominy. McClellan abandoned the siege, ordering his men back to defensive positions on the James. His priority was saving his army. Lee could not deliver a decisive blow. On June 29 the Union held off a Confederate attack at Savage's Station. Lee's army was bogged down in White Oak Swamp, and unable to prevent Union troops from retreating.

Lee's last chance to stop McClellan came at Malvern Hill on July 1. Despite facing a defensive position bolstered by more than 100 guns, Lee made a series of frontal assaults. Infantry charges were met by barrages of Union artillery fire that Confederate artillery was unable to counter. The battle ended in defeat for Lee and left his army exhausted. On July 2 the Army of the Potomac moved to safety at Harrison's Landing. Lee had saved the Confederate capital but in seven days had lost more than 20,000 men—a quarter of his army. McClellan had lost his chance to take Richmond. It was another two years before the Union forces were again this close to the Confederate capital.

Curriculum Context

It might be interesting to imagine how the impact of the war might have been different had it finished in summer 1862.

Campaign Details

The Union Army of the Potomac was only a few miles outside the Confederate capital, Richmond, when Confederate General Robert E. Lee seized the initiative and attacked an isolated Union corps north of the Chickahominy River on June 26 at Mechanicsville. In the next few days Lee's Army of Northern Virginia fought McClellan's army at Gaines' Mill, Savage's Station, Frayser's Farm, and Malvern Hill, as well as in numerous skirmishes. McClellan gave up his attempt to besiege Richmond and retreated to Harrison's Landing on the James River.

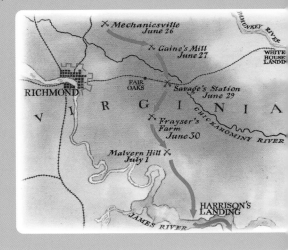

Shenandoah Valley Campaign

Virginia's Shenandoah Valley was strategically important as a source of crops and livestock and as a route by which Confederate forces could invade the North. As a result, both sides fought to control it throughout the Civil War.

The Shenandoah Valley, also called the Valley of Virginia, lies between the Allegheny Mountains and the Blue Ridge Mountains. During the Civil War it was the scene of numerous minor engagements and two major campaigns.

Jackson's Valley Campaign

The first major campaign pitted Confederate General Thomas J. "Stonewall" Jackson against several Union generals in spring 1862. Jackson's mission was to divert as many Union troops as possible from the Peninsular Campaign in Virginia, which he accomplished with some skill. At Kernstown on March 23 Jackson's force of just 4,500 men attacked a Union division of 9,000 men. Jackson was defeated, but the Lincoln administration assumed that he would only have attacked if he outnumbered the Union force. As a result, the Union stationed nearly 60,000 troops to protect the valley and the region around Washington, D.C.

The area's Union commander was Nathaniel P. Banks. By late April he had advanced as far as Harrisonburg. Then Jackson attacked in turn and defeated a Union force at McDowell on May 8. His army was increased to 17,000 by the addition of a division under Richard S. Ewell. With this combined force Jackson launched an attack at Front Royal on May 23, threatening Banks's supply line and forcing him to retreat.

The Confederates attacked again at Winchester on May 25, and the Union troops retreated in panic across the

Curriculum Context

The Union's vast over-estimate of the size of Jackson's forces is a good example of the importance of reliable intelligence during the war, and the difficulty of getting it.

Supply line

The route by which an army receives stores such as food and ammunition.

Curriculum Context

Some curricula might ask you to give specific examples of outstanding generalship during the war; Jackson's campaign is a good example.

Potomac River into Maryland. The Union gathered 35,000 troops to trap Jackson, but in two remarkable battles at Cross Keys and Port Republic on June 8 and 9 he defeated both forces before they could combine against him. Jackson then left the valley to join Robert E. Lee in the defense of Richmond. Jackson's Valley Campaign was a textbook example of how a smaller force can outmaneuver and outfight a larger one.

Campaign Details

Confederate General "Stonewall" Jackson's campaign in the Shenandoah Valley in spring 1862 had the aim of tying up as many Union troops as possible. He managed to move up and down the valley at great speed, confusing the Union command as to his strength and whereabouts. His army of just 17,000 outmaneuvered three Union forces with a combined strength of 64,000. He won five battles—Front Royal, McDowell, First Winchester, Cross Keys, and Port Republic—between May 8 and June 9, 1862.

Hunter in the valley

The Shenandoah Valley remained quiet for nearly two years, punctuated only by the Second Battle of Winchester on June 15, 1863, in which Lee's army captured 3,500 men during the Gettysburg Campaign. In 1864 the Valley once more saw major fighting. On May 15 a small Confederate army led by John C. Breckinridge routed a Union force under Franz Sigel at New Market. A few weeks later Union troops returned under David Hunter and overwhelmed a Confederate force at Piedmont on June 5. Hunter captured Staunton and continued to Lexington, where he burned the Virginia Military Institute. Lee was forced to send Jubal A. Early to deal with Hunter. Early's corps defeated Hunter and advanced as far as the outskirts of Washington, D.C., before being turned back.

Sheridan's campaign

Union General Ulysses S. Grant gave Philip H. Sheridan the task of beating Early and eliminating the valley as a source of supplies for the Confederacy. In an episode known as "the Burning," Sheridan's cavalry destroyed over 2,000 grain-filled barns and killed thousands of sheep, cattle, and hogs. Then, in three major battles—Third Winchester (September 19), Fisher's Hill (September 22), and Cedar Creek (October 19)—Sheridan all but wrecked Early's corps. These victories were important politically as well as militarily, helping ensure Lincoln's reelection as president in 1864.

Rout

To utterly defeat and force to scatter.

Curriculum Context

Students might be asked to evaluate the contrasting effects on public opinion in the North and the South of events such as "the Burning."

Shiloh, Battle of

The battle was fought on April 6–7, 1862, between Albert S. Johnston's Confederate forces and Union armies led by Ulysses S. Grant and Don Carlos Buell around Shiloh Church and Pittsburg Landing on the Tennessee River.

Henry and Donelson

The capture of the forts is described on pages 58–60.

In February 1862 General Ulysses S. Grant captured Forts Henry and Donelson, forcing Confederate General Albert S. Johnston to retreat. Securing these forts opened the way for Union forces to move south.

By March there were two Union armies poised to strike into Mississippi. Grant was in the lead, moving his army of 30,000 to Pittsburg Landing, 25 miles (40 km) north of Corinth, Mississippi, while an army of 50,000 men under Don Carlos Buell was in Nashville preparing to join him. In April Johnston tried to recapture western Tennessee and Nashville by launching an offensive from Corinth, hoping to defeat Grant before he could unite with Buell.

Curriculum Context

Control of the Tennessee and Mississippi Rivers was key to both sides in the war in the West.

Johnston assembled an army of 45,000 men with General Pierre G.T. Beauregard as his second in command. On April 3 he advanced toward Pittsburg Landing. He planned a surprise attack; but disorganization and bad weather slowed the Confederates down, and they arrived south of Grant's position on the night of April 5.

Surprise attack

Rebel yell

A long, high-pitched yell adopted by Confederate infantry when charging into battle.

The delay did not jeopardize Johnston's plan, because Grant had not posted lookouts around his army. The Union soldiers had no idea they faced a Southern army until about 5:00 A.M. on April 6, when thousands of men in gray charged out of the woods screaming the blood-curdling rebel yell. The Confederates first struck the Union right, attacking William T. Sherman's division

Battle Details

1. Albert S. Johnston's Confederates made a surprise attack early on April 6. They drove back Union troops from Shiloh Church but encountered stiff resistance at the "Hornet's Nest." In the early afternoon Johnston was killed, and Beauregard took command.

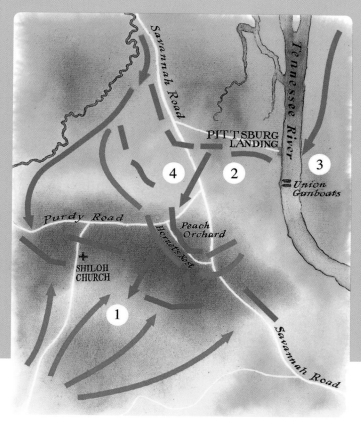

2. The Confederates pushed the Union troops back to the river by nightfall.

3. During the night the Union army was reinforced by forces under Buell.

4. On April 7 Buell counterattacked. The Confederates fought doggedly, but the Union troops made steady progress. In the late afternoon Beauregard ordered the Confederate forces to withdraw to Corinth.

at Shiloh Church. They then attacked the Union center, pushing three divisions back across Purdy Road. Southern reinforcements forced Sherman's men back to the Savannah Road by 10:00 A.M.

The Union right was in retreat, but Generals Hurlburt and Prentiss held their ground on the center and left of the Union line in and around a peach orchard for nearly five hours. The buzzing noise of bullets gave Prentiss's

Curriculum Context

Some curricula may expect students to be familiar with famous specific incidents of the war, such as the fighting at the Hornets' Nest.

position the name "the Hornets' Nest." It was the scene of some of the fiercest hand-to-hand fighting in the whole war.

By early afternoon Johnston had three of his four corps in the fight. But Union resistance at the Peach Orchard and Hornets' Nest warned him that his own right flank might be threatened, so he ordered forward his reserve corps. Soon afterward he was fatally wounded, and command passed to Beauregard.

As Union troops were desperately holding the line, Grant was organizing reinforcements. One division advanced from the north to support Sherman, and three of Buell's divisions were also on their way. The Union position came close to collapse, and retreating soldiers crowded around Pittsburg Landing. Prentiss actually surrendered at about 5:30 P.M. Had the Confederates pressed home their attack, they might have swept away Grant's army. But they were exhausted after 14 hours of fighting, and at 7:00 P.M. they stopped for the night to rest.

Second day of battle

The respite gave Grant a chance to stabilize his army. During the night Buell's divisions crossed the river, artillery was concentrated above Pittsburg Landing, and gunboats fired on Confederate positions. The Union counterattacked early on April 7. The Confederates lost all the ground they had won the day before and retreated to Corinth. The battle, one of the bloodiest of the conflict, cost the South 10,700 killed and wounded for no gain at all, while the North narrowly avoided defeat at a cost of 13,000 casualties.

South Mountain, Battle of

The Battle of South Mountain was fought on September 14, 1862, during the Confederate invasion of Maryland. Although it was overshadowed by the much bloodier battle at Antietam three days later, the engagement was crucial.

When Confederate General Robert E. Lee's Army of Northern Virginia crossed the Potomac River into Maryland in early September 1862, Union General George B. McClellan pursued.

Plugging the gaps

McClellan planned to push through three passes in South Mountain: Crampton's Gap, Fox's Gap, and Turner's Gap. He would engage Lee's army and send troops to relieve Harpers Ferry. Warned of McClellan's pursuit, Lee gathered his army at Sharpsburg. He ordered a division under Daniel H. Hill to defend a ridge along South Mountain to the east. The Union VI Corps struck at Crampton's Gap, easily defeating a thin Confederate defensive line. At dusk a Confederate counterattack slowed the Union assault and condemned Harpers Ferry to capture. The fighting at Fox's and Turner's Gaps was equally frustrating for Union troops. Hill's brigades blocked the gaps until nightfall, as Union General Ambrose E. Burnside committed troops of I and IX Corps in a piecemeal fashion, allowing Hill time to shift his defenses and make way for reinforcements. As night fell, the Union army had opened Crampton's and Fox's Gaps, but Longstreet's men blocked Turner's Gap until dawn.

Despite the Union victory at South Mountain, Hill's defense delayed the Union for a crucial day. The Army of the Potomac would now have to face a reunited Army of Northern Virginia on the banks of Antietam Creek near Sharpsburg.

Piecemeal
Bit by bit, rather than according to an overall plan.

Antietam
Follow the story of Antietam on pages 8–12.

Spotsylvania, Battle of

The Battle of Spotsylvania, Virginia, fought on May 8–19, 1864, was the second battle in the Overland Campaign of General Ulysses S. Grant. Days of bitter fighting resulted in more than 12,000 Confederate and 18,000 Union casualties.

Wilderness

Read about the battle on pages 102–103

Salient

A bulge in a defensive line that faces the enemy on three sides.

Curriculum Context

The story of the oak tree at the Bloody Angle is a good detail to include to indicate how intense gunfire could become during Civil War battles.

After the inconclusive Battle of the Wilderness (May 5–7, 1864), General Ulysses S. Grant and the Union Army of the Potomac attempted to move south and east toward Richmond, the Confederate Capital.

Both armies emerged from the Wilderness woodlands on the night of May 7, but the Confederates got to Spotsylvania first. Lee established a defensive line north of the village, but his position had one weakness—a bulge, or salient, where his line followed high ground. Following inconclusive attacks, Union Colonel Emory Upton led an assault on this salient, temporarily piercing Confederate defenses. Grant attacked again on the 12th, achieving another breakthrough and taking almost an entire division of Lee's army. The Confederates plugged the gap. A day of hand-to-hand combat in pouring rain followed.

Desperate fighting

This fight at the "Bloody Angle" was among the most desperate of the war. An oak tree 20 inches (50 cm) thick was sawn down by bullets, and thousands of killed and wounded soldiers littered the earthworks. Bold Confederate counterattacks eventually restored the situation, but Lee was convinced of the need to withdraw to a stronger position. He began to do so on May 14, and subsequent attacks by both armies on different parts of this new line were unsuccessful. Inconclusive fighting continued until May 19, when Grant disengaged to move east. Like the Battle of the Wilderness, Spotsylvania had ended in a draw.

Sumter, Fort

On April 12, 1861, the first shots of the war were fired on the Union-held Fort Sumter in Charleston Harbor, South Carolina. The incident transformed a small fort into a place of enduring symbolic significance to both sides.

Once the Confederacy was declared, President Jefferson Davis faced a diplomatic crisis. He could not allow the Union to retain a garrison in the heart of Confederate territory. He was also concerned that secessionists in South Carolina may seize the fort on their own initiative. Whatever Davis decided to do about the fort, war with the Union was inevitable.

The first shots

At 3:20 A.M. on April 12 Confederate Colonel James Chesnut and Captain Stephen D. Lee made a final demand for the fort's surrender. Its commander, Major Anderson, refused, believing backup troops and supplies would arrive imminently. The Confederates warned that shelling would start within the hour, and at 4:30 A.M. the first shell was fired. The Union troops were short of ammunition and so fired only occasional rounds from a few of their guns.

Fort Sumter falls

Confederate batteries resumed heavy shelling at dawn on April 13. The barracks inside the fort caught fire, and the defenders lay on the ground to escape the smoke. Anderson conceded defeat: The first engagement of the Civil War had ended in a Confederate victory.

Fort Sumter remained in Confederate hands for much of the war, creating a weak point in the Union blockade. The Union made repeated failed attempts to retake the fort, but the Confederates did not evacuate it until February 17, 1865.

Curriculum Context

Many curricula ask students to understand the significance of Fort Sumter as the first military action of the Civil War.

Blockade

A system of warships and coastal defenses the Union used to prohibit Confederate marine trade.

Surrender of the Confederacy

General Robert E. Lee's surrender of the Army of Northern Virginia to General Ulysses S. Grant on April 9, 1865, was not the end of the Confederacy, despite popular belief. It took several more weeks for the Civil War to come to an end.

Appomattox

Learn how the two men had come to Appomattox on pages 13–15.

Curriculum Context

Students may be asked to summarize some of the different views of the surrender in the North and the South.

Although Grant and Lee were the generals-in-chief of all the Union and Confederate armies fighting across the country, neither of them had the political authority to enable them to conclude a nationwide peace and end the war. The talks the two soldiers held at Appomattox Court House dealt only with the surrender of Lee's army in Virginia. President Abraham Lincoln had made it clear to Grant early in 1865 that national peace was a political question to be resolved between the Union government and the seceded states and was the sole responsibility of the president. In addition, there could be no talks about the surrender of the Confederacy as a nation because Lincoln and his administration had never accepted the Confederacy's claim that it was a separate country nor recognized the legitimacy of President Jefferson Davis's government.

Peace would come when each of the seceded states returned to the Union and accepted the terms on which that Union was now based, notably the Thirteenth Amendment of January 1865, which abolished slavery. That, however, depended on the surrender of all the Confederate armies. After the fall of Richmond, which sent the Confederate government on the run in North Carolina, the armies were the only thing holding the South together.

The surrender at Appomattox

The surrender of the Army of Northern Virginia took three days. The first meeting between Lee and Grant took place in the parlor of Wilbur McLean's farmhouse in the village of Appomattox Court House on April 9. Here Lee agreed to Grant's terms. They were then written down in the form of a letter to Lee, which the Confederate general acknowledged with a written note of acceptance.

Terms
The conditions on which a victor accepts a surrender.

There was little sense of triumph among the men of the victorious Union army when the news of Lee's surrender spread on April 9. Someone organized a celebratory 100-gun salute; but when Grant heard of it, he ordered it stopped. As he later explained in his memoirs, "The Confederates were now our prisoners, and we did not want to exult over their downfall."

The surrender of the Army of Northern Virginia left three major Confederate forces in the field: the army of General Joseph E. Johnston in North Carolina, that of General Richard Taylor in eastern Louisiana, Alabama, and Mississippi, and General Edmund Kirby Smith's Army of the Trans-Mississippi in an area west of the Mississippi River.

A drawing by Alfred Waud of Union General George A. Custer (center) accepting a flag of truce from a defeated Confederate officer in April 1865. Custer's cavalry had played an important role in forcing the retreat of the Army of Northern Virginia in the first week of April 1865.

Other surrenders

On April 17 and 18 Johnston met with Union General William T. Sherman and agreed to a surrender. However, new Union President Andrew Johnson refused to ratify it, since it dealt with political issues, such as the recognition of existing Southern state governments. Grant was sent to North Carolina to get Sherman to renegotiate.

On April 26 Johnston signed a new surrender document dealing strictly with military matters in line with the terms agreed upon at Appomattox. His men were to surrender their arms and return home, and no action would be taken against them by the United States.

By this time Richard Taylor was discussing terms with Union General Edward R.S. Canby, while Union General John Pope in New Orleans had written to his opposite number, Kirby Smith, suggesting surrender. Kirby Smith, however, was under pressure from politicians and his own junior officers to fight on. Confederate governors from Arkansas, Louisiana, and Missouri, and a subordinate officer, General "Jo" Shelby, wanted him to continue the war, as did Jefferson Davis, who had fled with the remaining members of the Confederate government from Richmond, Virginia, into Georgia. Davis hoped to cross the Mississippi River and continue the war in the West, despite advice from the military that further resistance would be useless.

Final capitulation

Most of the remnants of the Confederacy's military forces finally gave up their fight in May. Canby took Taylor's surrender in Alabama, Southern forces were surrendering in Florida and Arkansas, and on May 10 Jefferson Davis was captured by Union cavalry in Georgia. By the end of the month Union officers were in talks with Kirby Smith, and on June 2 he

Ceremony of Surrender

After Lee's surrender at Appomattox there seemed to be a sense of loss among many Union soldiers. This feeling was evident on April 12, when the Army of Northern Virginia marched out for the last time to lay down its arms and battle flags at a ceremony of formal surrender.

"On they came," wrote Union General Joshua L. Chamberlain, "with the same old swinging route step and swaying battle flags. In the van[guard], the proud Confederate ensign. . . . Before us in proud humiliation stood the embodiment of manhood; men whom neither toils or sufferings, not the fact of death, nor disaster, nor hopelessness could bend from their resolve; standing before us now, thin, worn, and famished, but erect, and with eyes looking level into ours, waking memories that bound us together as no other bond."

As the Confederates came down the Union lines, bugles ordered the men in blue to "carry arms," a salute to their enemy which the Southerners gallantly responded to, "honor answering honor," in Chamberlain's words. It was a worthy end to the hard-fought war in Virginia.

surrendered the Army of the Trans-Mississippi at Galveston, Texas. On June 23, in Indian Territory, the Cherokee commander Stand Watie became the last Confederate general to surrender his command. It had taken seven weeks from Lee's surrender at Appomattox for the last Confederate force to lay down its arms.

The Confederacy was gone, but some diehards refused to accept surrender, including Jo Shelby, who took 600 men with him into Mexico to try to find a way to continue the struggle.

On June 6 the first Confederate prisoners of war who were willing to take the oath of allegiance to the United States began to be released. On June 10 President Johnson started the process of appointing new governors for the former Confederate states, beginning with Mississippi and Georgia. Despite this rapid move toward peace and reconciliation, it was not until August 20, 1866, that Johnson officially declared the Civil War was over, proclaiming that "The insurrection is at an end."

Stand Watie

The Cherokee chief Stand Watie was the most senior Native American officer in the Confederate armies.

Curriculum Context

You might be asked to describe the feelings of the Southern soldiers who took the oath of allegiance.

Vicksburg, Siege of

The capture of Vicksburg, Mississippi, was essential for the Union to regain control of the Mississippi River. Union General Ulysses S. Grant's campaign to take the Confederate stronghold lasted from December 1862 until July 1863.

Curriculum Context

You might be asked to describe the reasons for Vicksburg's strategic importance to the Confederacy.

Located on well defended high bluffs on a loop in the river, the fortress city of Vicksburg dominated the trade of a vast area between New Orleans and Memphis. By June 1862 both cities had fallen. Vicksburg was the only city linking the two halves of the Confederacy. If it fell, the Confederacy would split in two. President Jefferson Davis ordered it to be held at all costs.

In December 1862 Grant planned a two-part assault on Vicksburg from the north. William T. Sherman would sail down the Mississippi River and land north of Vicksburg near the Yazoo River, while Grant would march overland from Memphis. Grant was halted when Confederate raiders destroyed his main supply base at Holly Springs, Mississippi. Sherman withdrew on the 29th, after he failed to capture high bluffs north of the city. The Mississippi protected the city to the west, and so Grant hoped to maneuver his army through the flooded lowland swamps, ferry it across the river, and attack from the high ground to the east. Through the winter he made three attempts to get the army in behind Vicksburg using river transport. They all failed.

Curriculum Context

The role of the Mississippi and its swamps in protecting Vicksburg is a good example of how geography influenced the course of the war.

A daring strategy

At the end of March Grant changed tactics. He ordered the army to cut its way through the swamps about 30 miles (50 km) to the south. Meanwhile Union gunboats under David D. Porter successfully met with Grant's army. On April 30 gunboats transported the Union forces to the east bank, while Sherman made a diversionary attack north of the city.

Once across the river, Grant marched east. Moving rapidly and living off the land, Grant's army met with Johnston's army at Jackson on May 14 and drove it back. Grant then turned west to advance on Pemberton's army in front of Vicksburg. On May 16 Grant defeated Pemberton at Champion's Hill and the next day at Big Black River. Pemberton retreated into Vicksburg on May 18, and after two failed assaults on May 19 and 22 Grant besieged the city.

Vicksburg under siege

The Union army dug 15 miles (24 km) of trenches and brought up 220 heavy guns to bombard the city day and night. Inside Vicksburg civilians suffered as badly from the shelling as the soldiers. Pemberton was reluctant to give in. He tried to negotiate with Grant, but Grant would accept only unconditional surrender. On July 4, 1863, Pemberton surrendered Vicksburg, and Grant's troops entered the city.

Living off the land
Traveling without supplies and relying on whatever food and drink it came across.

Battle Details

In March–April 1863 General Grant took his army down the Union-held Louisiana side of the Mississippi River and crossed the river at Bruinsburg with 30,000 men in David Porter's fleet of troop transports.

The Union army then moved eastward, fighting a number of battles on the way, and captured Jackson, the state capital of Mississippi on May 14. Grant then turned toward Vicksburg and defeated Pemberton's troops at Champion's Hill and Big Black River before besieging the city. Finally, Pemberton surrendered on July 4, 1863.

West, War in the

The western theater was the war's decisive theater. Although the eastern theater grabbed most of the headlines, with few exceptions the war's most sweeping and important campaigns were fought in the West.

Curriculum Context

Many curricula expect students to be able to summarize the main events of the war in the West.

The western theater encompassed Kentucky and Tennessee, most of Mississippi and Alabama, and part of Louisiana—everything between the Mississippi River and the Appalachian Mountains. The fighting here was so fierce by 1864 the western Union armies had carried the struggle to the Appalachian Mountains and into Georgia. By the end of 1864 the western theater could be said to extend all the way to the Atlantic Ocean.

Neutrality

Not participating in or taking sides in a conflict.

The west saw little fighting in 1861. Kentucky's neutrality helped keep Union and Confederate forces apart. In September 1861 the rival armies entered the state. Confederates occupied a line across the lower part of the state from Columbus on the Mississippi to the Cumberland Gap in the Appalachian foothills. Union troops seized Smithland, Louisville, Frankfort, and Lexington, with more Union troops in Cairo, Illinois.

Defensive line broken

The first encounter in the West was on January 19, 1862, when a small Union army routed a Confederate force at the Battle of Mill Springs breaking the eastern end of the Confederacy's defensive line in the west. A few weeks later, a combined Union land and naval force captured Forts Henry and Donelson. The loss broke the center of the Confederate line, and Albert S. Johnston, the Confederate commander in the western theater, ordered a withdrawal. Within days the capital of Tennessee, Nashville, fell into Union hands without a fight. By the end of March Union forces were at Pittsburg Landing near the Tennessee–Mississippi state

Henry and Donelson

The capture of the forts is described on pages 58–60.

line. Their objective was the key railroad junction at Corinth, Mississippi. In early April Johnston took the offensive, hoping to destroy the Union army at Pittsburg Landing before additional Northern troops arrived. The battle, known as Shiloh or Pittsburg Landing (April 6–7), was one of the bloodiest of the war. On the first day the Confederates almost won; but Johnston was killed, and his inexperienced troops became disorganized. The Union commander, Grant, ordered a counterattack on the second day, forcing a Confederate retreat. Within weeks more than 100,000 Union troops had gathered at Pittsburg Landing under the overall command of Henry W. Halleck. By the end of May, after a cautious advance, Halleck captured Corinth. He then dispersed his army to consolidate his grip on the Union gains of the spring campaign.

Shiloh
The battle is described on pages 86–88.

The struggle for the Mississippi

In April 1862 the Union took New Orleans at the mouth of the river on the Gulf coast. The Confederates soon lost control of the river except for a 200-mile (320-km) stretch from Vicksburg, Mississippi, south to Port Hudson, Louisiana. Grant's Army of the Tennessee made the first attempt to capture Vicksburg in November–December 1862. Within weeks it had to turn back after Confederates destroyed its forward supply base. The swampland north of Vicksburg made it almost impossible to attack from there, so in April 1863 Grant ordered Union gunboats and transports to run the Vicksburg batteries by night. He marched his army to link up with the Union flotilla, which ferried his troops to the Mississippi side. In a brilliant campaign Grant fought a series of battles that isolated Vicksburg. After a 47-day siege the city fell on July 4. Port Hudson surrendered within a week.

The Confederate defensive line at the beginning of the war stretched from the Mississippi River to the Cumberland Gap in the Appalachian foothills. The strategic importance of the rivers and railroads in the west meant that many major battles were fought in the western theater.

The Union campaign for Tennessee

After the capture of Nashville in March 1862 and Memphis, which fell after a brief naval battle on June 6, 1862, the only major cities in Tennessee still in Confederate hands were Knoxville and Chattanooga, a critical rail center. Union General Don Carlos Buell spent the early summer of 1862 in a slow advance toward Chattanooga repairing the railroad as he went.

Union troops of the 5th Ohio Infantry enter Memphis on June 6, 1862, the day the port city fell to the Union after a naval battle on the Mississippi, which was watched by the civilian population from the bluffs overlooking the river.

Confederate General Braxton Bragg began an offensive from Chattanooga toward Kentucky, forcing Buell to abandon all of mid-Tennessee except Nashville. He retreated to Louisville on the Ohio River before turning east to confront Bragg in central Kentucky. Elements of the two armies clashed at Perryville on October 8. Although Bragg's army did well, he realized he had defeated only part of Buell's force and retreated, ending his invasion of Kentucky. Unhappy with Buell's performance, the Lincoln administration replaced him with William S. Rosecrans.

Rosecrans advanced from Nashville in December 1862 and met Bragg's army in the savage Battle of Stone's River, near Murfreesboro, Tennessee (December 31, 1862–January 2, 1863). Rosecrans won, but at such a cost his army spent the next six months recovering. Finally, at the end of June Rosecrans resumed his advance, outmaneuvered Bragg, and captured Chattanooga without a fight on September 9. As Rosecrans continued his advance into northern Georgia, Bragg's army was reinforced. Bragg surprised Rosecrans in the Battle of Chickamauga (September 19–20). He forced the Union army back into Chattanooga, occupied the high ridges south and east of the city, cutting off the Union army from resupply. It seemed the Union army would be starved into

Murfreesboro
Read about the battle on page 69.

Chickamauga
More details on pages 38–39.

surrender until Grant was given overall command in the western theater in October 1863. He sent reinforcements; and on November 25 the Union army at Chattanooga defeated Bragg's army, which withdrew into Georgia. Joseph E. Johnston replaced Bragg. By the spring of 1864 Grant was the overall Union commander. His successor in command of the western theater was William T. Sherman. Grant ordered Sherman to break up Johnston's army and target Confederate war resources. Sherman launched an offensive against Atlanta, Georgia, an important rail center and a major industrial city. For three months Johnston parried Sherman's maneuvers but fell back steadily until the Confederate government replaced him with John Bell Hood. Hood made a series of attacks on Sherman but failed to push him away from Atlanta. On September 2 the city fell to the Union.

Curriculum Context

Students tracing the career of Ulysses S. Grant should include his decisive contribution in the western theater in fall 1863.

Atlanta

Read more about the fall of Atlanta and its crucial political impact on pages 16–18.

Final campaigns

The capture of Atlanta elated the North. Hood tried to cut Sherman's supply line but failed. On November 21 he embarked on a disastrous invasion of Tennessee that came to grief in the Battle of Nashville (December 15–16). Hood's invasion cleared the way for Sherman to carry out his March to the Sea, an operation intended to secure a new supply base on the Atlantic coast but famous for its destruction. Johnston, belatedly restored to command, could not stop him and on April 26, 1865, surrendered to Sherman near Raleigh, North Carolina.

March to the Sea

The story of Sherman's notorious campaign is told on pages 63–66.

War in the Far West

In addition to the western theater the Civil War also saw minor operations in the far West. The most important was a Confederate attempt to seize New Mexico Territory in early 1862. Troops under Henry Hopkins Sibley advanced up the Rio Grande Valley in January 1862 and won an early success at Valverde, New Mexico, on February 21. They were forced to turn back after their supplies were destroyed by E.R.S. Canby's forces after a clash at Glorieta Pass, New Mexico, on March 28.

Wilderness, Battle of the

On May 5 and 6, 1864, General Robert E. Lee's Confederate Army of Northern Virginia fought the Union Army of the Potomac under General Ulysses S. Grant in a densely wooded part of Virginia known as the Wilderness.

Chancellorsville

Read about the Union defeat on pages 32–34.

Grant wanted to fight Lee's army on open ground. To do that, his 120,000-strong army first had to get through the Wilderness—a marshy area of dense woodland and scrub where the Union had suffered a terrible defeat at the Battle of Chancellorsville.

On May 4 Union troops moved into the Wilderness. When Lee learned of their presence, he decided to attack, knowing the Wilderness's thick undergrowth would neutralize Grant's superior numbers.

Confederate attack

The battle began early on May 5 with Confederate attacks along the Orange Turnpike and Plank Road. The fighting was chaotic. The two sides were barely yards apart in places but were hidden from one another by thick undergrowth and clouds of smoke from musket fire. Exploding shells started fires that raged unchecked burning hundreds of helpless wounded men to death. The battle continued all day, but Union forces held on and by nightfall were in a position to attack Lee's right.

Curriculum Context

Students describing the experience of battle for ordinary soldiers could mention the chaotic conditions at the Battle of the Wilderness.

Second day of battle

At dawn on May 6 both sides attacked again. By 7:00 A.M. Union forces were about to break the Confederate line when Longstreet's troops, which had arrived overnight, counterattacked. With Union troops in retreat, Longstreet took advantage of his men's local knowledge to mount a surprise attack. The Union troops were caught off guard, and the Confederates were soon able to push back the Union left, but their

Battle Details

On May 4 Union troops entered the Wilderness along the Germanna Plank Road and across Ely's Ford. On May 5 the battle began when troops under Confederate General Richard S. Ewell attacked along the Orange Turnpike. Confederate General Ambrose P. Hill attacked down the Orange Plank Road. Hill was unable to break through. Fighting continued in the dense undergrowth until evening. On May 6 the battle was renewed. Union troops were about to break the Confederate line when reserves counterattacked. More Union reserves arrived in the afternoon, and fighting continued until nightfall. The battle ended in a tactical draw, but was a strategic victory for the Union, as Grant continued to march south.

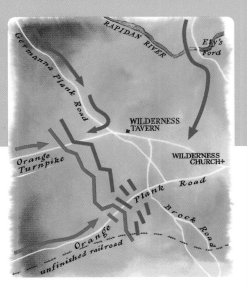

attack stalled in thick undergrowth. Longstreet's corps became muddled with Hill's, and Longstreet was shot and seriously wounded by one of his own side. He survived, but was out of action for several months.

Union reinforcements

By late afternoon fresh troops arrived on the Union line. Grant ordered a new attack, but Lee struck first with a frontal assault over Union breastworks. Darkness ended the fighting on the Plank Road, but it suddenly flared again north of the Orange Turnpike with a Confederate attack on the Union right. However, Grant's refusal to be overawed by Lee's reputation and the arrival of fresh reserves stopped the rout.

Breastworks

A temporary earthwork of about chest height, built as a fortification.

The inconclusive battle cost Lee 8,700 casualties. Grant's army suffered 17,000 dead and wounded, but the heavy losses did not shake his resolve. For the first time, Grant ordered his troops to continue the advance south toward Spotsylvania. Lee did not shake off Grant until the day he surrendered at Appomattox.

Winchester, Battles of

Winchester, Virginia, was strategically located at the northern end of the Shenandoah Valley at an important road and rail intersection. The town saw numerous small engagements as well as three significant battles in the Civil War.

Winchester lay on an invasion route, which either side might use. It offered an entry into the Shenandoah Valley, one of the Confederacy's most productive agricultural regions. The first battle was on May 25, 1862, on the hills southwest of the town. It was part of Confederate General Thomas J. "Stonewall" Jackson's Shenandoah Valley Campaign to divert Union forces from reinforcing General George B. McClellan's Army of the Potomac. Jackson's Confederates attacked Union General Nathaniel P. Banks's troops so fiercely they broke ranks and fled north.

The second battle

The second battle of Winchester was fought on June 14–15, 1863, during the Confederate Army of Northern Virginia's invasion of Pennsylvania. Confederate General Richard S. Ewell's II Corps attacked a Union garrison from the Army of the Potomac led by General Robert H. Milroy. The Confederates' victory cleared a path for their invasion.

The third battle

The third battle took place east of Winchester on September 19, 1864. It was a key engagement of Union General Philip H. Sheridan's Shenandoah Valley Campaign against General Jubal A. Early. Outnumbered almost three to one, the Confederates fought all day, but their lines eventually broke. After losing nearly a quarter of his men, Early retreated through the town. Sheridan won another victory at Fisher's Hill, which kept Winchester in Union hands for the rest of the war.

Yorktown, Siege of

Yorktown, Virginia, near the tip of the peninsula between the York and James rivers, was besieged for four weeks by Union forces under George B. McClellan at the start of the Peninsular Campaign in the spring of 1862.

Confederate General John B. Magruder, with 13,000 troops, was defending Yorktown. On March 24, 1862, he notified Confederate authorities of the presence of Union troops on the peninsula. They were part of a 100,000-invading army led by McClellan, who planned to move up the peninsula to the Confederate capital, Richmond. Only Magruder's force was in the way, manning defensive lines across the peninsula between the York and James rivers. In early April McClellan began to advance on Yorktown. Confederate President Jefferson Davis ordered General Joseph E. Johnston to move his army of 53,000 from northern Virginia to the peninsula in mid-April.

Magruder was able to deceive McClellan as to the strength of his forces by marching his troops back and forth, creating the impression there were many more of them. This led the Union intelligence chief, Allan Pinkerton, to report wildly exaggerated numbers. McClellan, an engineer and cautious by nature, decided to besiege Yorktown rather than launch a direct assault.

Confederate evacuation

On April 17 Johnston took charge of the Confederate defenses. He convinced Davis of the need to withdraw before McClellan could use his vast superiority in men and guns to force a battle. The withdrawal began on the night of May 4, and Norfolk was evacuated soon after. Johnston moved west toward Richmond, occupying defenses at Williamsburg ready for the next phase of the Peninsular Campaign.

Peninsula

The aims of McClellan's Peninsular Campaign are described on pages 72–74.

Curriculum Context

Magruder's deception was just one of a number of examples of commanders being able to fool the enemy about the strength of their forces.

Glossary

abolition Ending slavery.

at all hazards At any cost.

battery An artillery unit, consisting of a number of guns and their crews.

blockade A system of warships and coastal defenses the Union used to prohibit Confederate maritime trade.

blockade-runner A sailor or ship that ran through the Union blockade of Southern ports during the Civil War.

bombard To subject to a sustained artillery attack.

breastworks Temporary earthworks of about chest height, built as a fortification.

brigade A military unit consisting of between two and six regiments, or around 5,000 soldiers; the brigade was the common tactical unit of the Civil War.

casualty A soldier lost in battle through death, wounds, sickness, capture, or missing in action.

cavalry Mounted soldiers; the role of cavalry changed considerably during the course of the war.

company A military unit consisting of 50 to 100 men commanded by a captain. There were 10 companies in a regiment. Companies were raised by individual states.

corps The largest military unit in the Civil War armies, consisting of two or more divisions. Corps were established in the Union army in March 1862 and in the Confederate army in November 1862.

counterattack To attack the enemy after it has attacked you.

crossfire Enemy fire coming from both sides at the same time.

deploy To arrange soldiers in formation ready for battle.

diversionary Actions intended to divert the enemy from a major military action.

division The second largest military unit in the Civil War armies. A division was made up of three or four brigades and was commanded by a brigadier or major general. There were between two and four divisions in a corps.

Dixie An unofficial anthem of the Confederacy; Dixie was an 1850s' popular song in which a freed slave looks back to the idealized plantation of his childhood.

draft A system of compulsory military service.

draft In shipping, the depth of a boat that is under the water.

enlist To join the military services.

entrench To dig in to defensive positions.

flank The exposed right or left-hand wing of an army.

flotilla A small naval unit or one or two squadrons of warships.

foragers Groups of soldiers who collected food and other supplies but did not pay for them.

garrison A unit of soldiers guarding a town or other stronghold.

guerrilla warfare Warfare that takes place through small-scale engagements, ambushes, and sabotage, rather than through set battles.

infantry Foot soldiers.

ironclad A new type of warship that was protected by an outer skin of iron armor.

line of communication The means by which commanders keep in touch with their armies by telegraph or messengers.

living off the land Traveling without supplies and relying on whatever food and drink one comes across.

maneuvers The coordinated movement of soldiers on the battlefield; infantry learned how to maneuver by constant repetition of drill to practice coordinated movements.

mine Known during the Civil War as "torpedoes," mines are explosive devices, usually concealed, designed to destroy enemy soldiers and transportation.

mortar A type of short-barreled cannon that threw shells in a high arc over enemy fortifications, commonly used in siege warfare.

neutral Not taking sides.

outflank To go around the side of an opposing force.

pillage To loot and plunder.

political appointee A military officer given his commission early in the war because of his social position or political loyalties rather than for his military skill.

pontoon bridges Temporary bridges, which often float on moored boats, or pontoons.

private The lowest rank in an army.

rebel yell A long, high-pitched yell adopted by Confederate infantry when charging into battle.

recruit A soldier or other serviceman who has just joined the services.

regiment A military unit consisting of 10 companies of 100 men at full strength. In practice, most Civil War regiments were much smaller than this. Raised by state governors, they were usually composed of men from the same area. The Civil War soldier's main loyalty and sense of identity was connected to his regiment.

review A formal military ceremony in which forces are reviewed by an important person.

rifling A technique used on both guns and cannons that allowed weapons to fire further and with greater accuracy than previously. Rifled barrels had spiral grooves cut into the inside, which gave a bullet or shell spin when fired.

rout An indisciplined and panicked retreat as soldiers flee for their lives.

salient A bulge in a defensive line that faces the enemy on three sides.

segregation The separation of people based on their skin color or another quality.

sentry A soldier standing guard.

siege To surround and cut off supplies to an army or town to force surrender.

skirmish A minor fight.

skirmishers Infantrymen trained to fight in open order rather than the closed ranks of ordinary soldiers. They were often used ahead of the main force to prepare the way for a main attack or as snipers to harass an enemy counterattack.

stalemate A deadlock in which neither side can gain an advantage.

strategic Important as part of an overall military plan.

strike colors To lower one's flag as an indication of surrender.

supply line The route by which an army receives stores such as food and ammunition.

small arms Weapons that are carried and fired by hand.

terms The conditions on which a victor accepts a surrender.

treason A crime against the government of one's own country.

ultimatum A final demand that, if not met, will result in punishment or war.

unconditional surrender A surrender where terms are dictated by the victors and are not subject to negotiation.

volunteer A civilian who fights when his country goes to war, often because of personal convictions, a sense of adventure, or for a bounty or enlistment fee. The majority of Civil War soldiers were volunteers, rather than regular soldiers.

Further Research

BOOKS

Barney, William L. *The Oxford Encyclopedia of the Civil War*. Oxford University Press, 2011.

Catton, Bruce. *The Civil War*. Boston, MA: Houghton Mifflin, 1987.

Civil War Preservation Trust. *Civil War Sites: The Official Guide to the Civil War Discovery Trail*. Globe Pequot, 2007.

Coles, David J., et al. *Encyclopedia of the American Civil War: Political, Social, and Military History*. W.W. Norton and Company, 2002.

Creighton, Margaret S. *The Colors of Courage: Gettysburg's Forgotten History: Immigrants, Women, and African Americans in the Civil War's Defining Battle*. Basic Books, 2006.

Engle, Stephen D. *The American Civil War: The War in the West 1861–July 1863*. London: Fitzroy Dearborn, 2001.

Gallagher, Gary W. *The American Civil War: The War in the East 1861–May 1863*. London: Fitzroy Dearborn, 2001.

Gallagher, Gary W., and Robert Krick. *The American Civil War: The War in the East 1863–1865*. London: Fitzroy Dearborn, 2001.

Glatthaar, Joseph T. *The American Civil War: The War in the West 1863–1865*. London: Fitzroy Dearborn, 2001.

Grant, Ulysses S. *Personal Memoirs*. New York: Crescent Books, 1995.

Hendrickson, Robert. *The Road to Appomattox*. New York: John Wiley, 1998.

Holzer, Harold, and Craig Symonds. *The New York Times Complete Civil War 1861–1865*. Black Dog and Leventhal Publishers, 2010.

Robertson, James I. *Soldiers Blue and Gray*. Columbia, SC: University of South Carolina Press, 1998.

Schindler, Stanley (editor). *Memoirs of Robert E. Lee*. New York: Crescent Books, 1994.

Sears, Stephen W. Gettysburg. Mariner Books, 2004.

Smith, Andrew F. *Starving the South: How the North Won the Civil War*. St. Martin's Press, 2011.

Smith, Gene. *Lee and Grant: A Dual Biography*. New York: McGraw-Hill, 1984.

Smith, Timothy B. The Untold Story of Shiloh: The Battle and the Battlefield. University of Tennessee Press, 2008.

Trudeau, Noah Andre. *Like Men of War: Black Troops in the Civil War, 1862–1865*. New York: Little, Brown, and Co, 1998.

Trudeau, Noah Andre. *Southern Storm: Sherman's March to the Sea*. Harper Perennial, 2009.

Trudeau, Noah Andre. *Gettysburg: A Testing of Courage*. Harper Perennial, 2003.

Wheeler, Richard. *Sword Over Richmond: An Eyewitness History of McClellan's Peninsula Campaign*. Books Sales, Inc., 2008.

Wheeler, Richard. *Lee's Terrible Swift Sword: From Antietam to Chancellorsville: An Eyewitness History*. Book Sales, Inc., 2008.

Wheeler, Richard. *Voices of the Civil War*. Plume, 1990.

Wiley, Bell Irvin. *The Life of Johnny Reb: The Common Soldier of the Confederacy*. Baton Rouge, LA: Louisiana State University Press, 1980.

Wiley, Bell Irvin. *The Life of Billy Yank: The Common Soldier of the Union*. Baton Rouge, LA: Louisiana State University Press, 1981.

Woodworth, Steven E. *Decision in the Heartland: The Civil War in the West*. Praeger, 2008.

Wortman, Marc. *The Bonfire: The Siege and Burning of Atlanta*. PublicAffairs, 2010.

INTERNET RESOURCES

These general sites have comprehensive links to a large number of Civil War topics:

http://sunsite.utk.edu/civil-war/warweb.html

http://civilwarhome.com/

http://americancivilwar.com/

http://www.civil-war.net/

http://www2.cr.nps.gov/abpp/battles/bystate.htm
This part of the National Parks Service site allows you to search for battles by state

http://pdmusic.org/civilwar.html
Sound files and words to Civil War songs

http://www.civilwarmed.org/
National Museum of Civil War Medicine

http://memory.loc.gov/ammem/aaohtml/exhibit/aopart4.html
Civil War section of the African American Odyssey online exhibition at the Library of Congress

http://valley.vcdh.virginia.edu/
The Valley of the Shadow Project: details of Civil War life in two communities, one Northern and one Southern

http://www.civilwarhome.com/records.htm
Battle reports by commanding generals from the Official Records

http://www.cwc.lsu.edu/
The United States Civil War Center at Lousiana State University

http://www.nps.gov/gett/gettkidz/soldslang.htm
Civil War slang from the site of the Gettysburg National Military Park

http://www.sonofthesouth.net/leefoundation/ebooks.htm
The Robert E. Lee Foundation digital library of books about Lee and about the Civil War generally

Index

Page numbers in *italic* refer to illustrations and captions.

Sharpsburg (Antietam), Battle of 8–12, 89
Shelby, "Jo" 94, 95
Shenandoah Valley 23, 72, 83–85, 104
Sheridan, Philip H. 40, 44, *45*, 79, 85, 104
Sherman, William T. 13, 16, 37, 61, 62, 63–66, 70, 80, 94, 96, 101
Shilo, Battle of 86–88, 99
Sickles, Daniel E. 53
Siege of Petersburg 44
signal flags 25
Smith, Kirby 94
South Carolina 65–66, 91
South Mountain, Battle of 89
Spotsylvania, Battle of 90
Stone's River, Battle of 69
Stuart, J.E.B. "Jeb" 19–21, 20, 21, 33, 51, 74, 81
Sudley Ford 24, 25
Sumter, Fort 91
supplies 13–14
surrender of the Confederacy 15, 92–95, 95

T

Taylor, Richard 94
Tennessee 37, 69, 70, 98, 100
    invasion of 101
Tennessee River 58, 59, *59*, 86
Thirteenth Amendment 92
Thomas, George H. 39, 70-71
total war 63

U

U.S. Army 6
USS *Hartford* 67

V

Vicksburg 55, 77, 99
    siege of 96–97
Virginia (ship) 56, 57, *57*
volunteers 7, 22

W

wagons *20*
Warren, Gouverneur K. 53
Washington, D.C. 25, 51

Watie, Isaac Stand 95
Waud, Alfred *93*
Weitzel, General 79
West, war in the 70, 98–101
    map *99*
Wilderness 32, 102–103
Wilderness, Battle of the 102–103
Winchester, battles of 83, 85, 104

Y

Yorktown 73
    siege of 105